S0-BSJ-500

Don Holm's Book of
FOOD DRYING, PICKLING AND SMOKE CURING

Also by Don Holm

The Complete Sourdough Cookbook
Old Fashioned Dutch Oven Cookbook
101 Best Fishing Trips in Oregon
Pacific North

Don Holm's Book of
FOOD DRYING,
PICKLING, &
SMOKE CURING

By

Don and Myrtle Holm

THE CAXTON PRINTERS, LTD.
CALDWELL, IDAHO
1992

First printing February, 1978
Second printing March, 1981
Third printing January, 1992

© 1978 by Donald R. Holm
All rights reserved

Library of Congress Cataloging in Publication Data

Holm, Don.
    Don Holm's book of Food drying, pickling & smoke
curing.

    Bibliography: p.
    1. Food, Dried. 2. Fish, Smoked. 3. Meat,
Smoked. 4. Canning and preserving. I. Holm, Myrtle,
joint author. II. Title. III. Title: Food drying,
pickling & smoke curing.
TX609.H64   641.4'4   75-28570
ISBN 0-87004-250-5

Lithographed and Bound in the United States of America by
The Caxton Printers, Ltd.
Caldwell, Idaho   83605
155399

To *Wild Rose*, for whom this book was written

My fare is really sumptuous this evening;
buffaloe's humps, tongues, and marrowbones,
fine trout, parched meal, pepper and salt,
and a good appetite. . . .

Capt. Meriwether Lewis,
on the Missouri River in Montana,
June, 1805

CONTENTS

INTRODUCTION

THERE IS A revolution in progress during this last quarter of the twentieth century.

It is not a political revolution; it is a revolution in eating and the preparation and preservation of the available foods in a shrinking world faced with the specter of overpopulation.

By the year A.D. 2000 there will be 50 million more Americans — and most of us already feel overcrowded in the middle 1970s. This will bring increased social and economic pressures, a closed-in feeling, and a great yearning to go back to a rural type of life — either in fact or vicariously. The urge is already upon most of us, whether we live in a Manhattan apartment or a mobile home in Arizona. In Oregon a community college offers a course in homesteading — and it is jam-packed each semester with people of all ages and economic status who want to learn how to gain five or ten acres and independence. Most of the students are dead serious and already have made down payments on small unimproved acreages.

The Census Bureau forecast also predicts shortages of everything, especially foods, as part of the general dwindling of resources. This and continued rising prices for supermarket goods make it more important that homemakers learn and routinely practice the old-time arts of preserving foods. This includes canning, drying, smoking, and pickling, as well as the modern technique of freezing and freeze-drying.

Most of us who came from a rural environment,

especially the Great Heartland of America, retain some fond recollections of life in those simplified times, when self-sufficiency was taken for granted and the center of the universe was the big kitchen with its grand old cast-iron stove that had a hot water reservoir and a warming oven, in addition to other forgotten wonders.

From this center of family life, at any given time of day, came the most heavenly aromas of fresh-baked sourdough bread, of wild berry preserves bubbling in a big pot, of stewing farm chickens. Even forty or fifty years later, just the thought of it brings back the taste and smell and feeling of security and goodness of life that most of us now think we have lost to technology and political strife.

Incidentally, the popular image of kids growing up today is one of artificial living and lack of parental companionship and guidance. The other day a survey was taken of grade school children in our community. They were asked what they considered the most important element of a good life in the future.

Know what the answer was, by an overwhelming percentage? The *family*. That is, the family unit, or environment. A sign of the gradual return to self-sufficiency and basic values.

Ironically, today we feel inward pangs of guilt here in America for a standard of living that has become so high most of us suffer from overweight and all its medical implications. At the same time that we worry about calories we also worry about rising costs — especially those of us who have to live on fixed incomes, those who are retired or about to retire, and those who just can't accept the pressures and demands of the rat race.

The current worldwide nostalgia kick — old movies, old books, old-style cooking — is a manifestation of all this. It isn't a fad; it is more than that. Maybe we're beginning to think that perhaps not all change is for the better and not all technology is progress.

There is a deep-running movement in all urban and

industrial countries for a return to basics, a complex inner dissatisfaction with too much sophistication. Man is a gregarious animal and will always seek companionship — but not necessarily crowds. Skyrise condominiums and regimented senior-citizen developments are becoming less alluring to retirees.

One can still be gregarious and neighborly in one of the thousands of small towns in America (most of which are actually losing population each year) where most of the advantages of the city are now available, without the smog and urban ills. There are still available family-type farms, unimproved acreages even in the crowded eastern states, nomadic trailer-home living, and that more recent vehicle of escape, the cruising houseboat.

To escape to the old ways does not necessarily mean you have to milk your own cows, spin your own yarn, and ride a horse to work. Young people today who are discovering the delights of bread baking, putting up food in mason jars, and smoking and pickling their own vegetables and meats, really have no comprehension of the godawful hard work many of us had to endure in the old days so mom could do this for the family. Today you don't necessarily have to endure a lot of drudgery. All the old kitchen skills that made for such wholesome nutritious eating in the good old days can be acquired and practiced just as well in today's modern kitchens and with modern appliances such as juice mills, blenders, grinders, electric flour mills, pressure retorts, portable smokers, and other devices. Moreover, we have available today such modern versions of the ancient Asian appliances as the Chinese *wok* and the Japanese *kamado*.

There's no reason why today we can't live just as simply as we did in those nostalgic years — or at least eat just as simply and certainly more wholesomely. With a little planning, some foresight, and a smattering of determination, we can live can live just as well for a lot less than we are spending.

With a little bit of planning and some practical help

from books such as this, we can beat the food cost spiral. We can even live off the land a little in most parts of the country, by making good use of the results of fishing and hunting trips, by shopping the farmer markets, and even by doing some gardening ourselves. Most people, even suburbanites, can raise all the vegetables they need for their own use. During the summer and fall thousands of miles of road right-of-way, even in populous states and especially in the West, are loaded with wild blackberries only a few steps from your car.

But there is more to it than all this. There is a challenge. A famous Harvard nutritionist, Prof. Jean Mayer, has written, "The same amount of food that is feeding 210 million Americans would feed 1.5 billion Chinese."

That is real food for thought. Half the people in the world go to bed hungry at night. The usable agricultural lands of the world are shriveling each year, while the population zooms. In many parts of the world the land is worn out, and there is a worldwide shortage of fertilizers. There is an apparent long-term change in weather patterns which will eventually affect every country and social system on earth. We now are plagued by widespread droughts.

A major change in life-style and eating habits is inevitable. This does not mean we will be eating less nourishing or less appetizing foods, but almost certainly we will be eating *less* food, one way or another.

For most of us this will be no great sacrifice. Most Americans today could get along very well on two-thirds or one-half of their present calorie intake and never feel hungry — if they had a properly balanced diet.

Back in the heat of World War II, when Americans and Allies were fighting their way back to the Philippines, some of the Japanese soldiers were cut off and isolated. Many were in hiding for years before they learned the war was over. A few remained in hiding because they could not accept surrender.

One of these was Lt. Hiro Onoda, who spent thirty

years in the mountains of Luzon before he was repatriated and returned to Japan in 1974. During his stay in the hospital Onoda amazed the doctors who performed more than two hundred tests on him. They discovered that, despite his ordeal, he was in far better physical condition than most Japanese living in a modern urban environment. His eyesight was exceptionally keen; his hearing was acute. He could drop off to sleep almost at will and awaken fully alert. He required only about four hours of sleep a night. His muscles were those of a young man, instead of a fifty-two year old. There was almost no subcutaneous fat on his body.

Although he lived by his wits, off the land, his diet was singularly balanced — meat from animals he killed, rice and vegetables stolen from farms, tree sprouts and wild leaves gathered in the jungle, wild nuts and berries. He kept himself scrupulously clean, treating any cuts or scratches with animal fat. He practiced moderation in everything — although he never gave up his smoking habit, being able to steal enough tobacco to keep puffing.

This was not an isolated case. Many of the Japanese soldiers who were repatriated after years in the jungle were found in similarly good physical condition.

In this book, as in our previous cookbooks such as *The Complete Sourdough Cookbook* and *The Old Fashioned Dutch Oven Cookbook* (The Caxton Printers, Ltd., Caldwell, Idaho), we have tried not to get carried away with Spartan ways but to deal with the more wholesome methods of cooking and preparing foods in a practical way that anyone can learn to master.

In this book we have carried out this theme and approach in greater detail as a logical extension of the others. Along with a complete section on drying and dehydrating, and on smoking and jerking, we are including a comprehensive treatise on practical pickling. After completing the research and writing of this, we were pleased to hear that members of the Pickle Packers International, during the annual Pickle Week, called on everyone to join the great pickle liberation movement.

The pickle, according to members, was being discriminated against "in every chauvinistic chicken and hamburger joint in the country." This despite the fact that about twenty billion pickles are eaten each year in the United States — which if placed end to end would stretch from Dill City, Oklahoma to Hamburg, Germany and back ninety-two times.

Moreover, the annual pickle bill in the United States comes to over $500 million. Clearly it is time to make room in books of this kind for the art and science of pickling.

Anyway, we tried to put this book together in such a way that you can have fun while you are becoming self-taught in the ancient and wonderful ways of Drying, Pickling, and Smoke Curing.

Don Holm's Book of
FOOD DRYING, PICKLING AND SMOKE CURING

I

DRYING YOUR OWN FOR FUN AND PROFIT

DRYING OR DEHYDRATING your own food at home fascinates, but at the same time mystifies, many folks who have not had rural beginnings. Actually it is so simple you will think there must be a trick to it. One of the first questions asked is, "what kinds of foods can I dehydrate?" The answer is, "anything you can eat, you can dehydrate." Dehydration means just that — removing the moisture. This also removes up to 75 percent of the volume or weight, depending on what kind of food it is. In this dried condition, the food will keep indefinitely without refrigeration or other processing. After drying, the food can then be eaten as is or reconstituted (by adding water) and used in various recipes and dishes just as the fresh food is.

That, in one paragraph, comprises the basics of food drying. The advantages and implications of this food-processing method are immediately obvious to the food grower, the homemaker, the outdoorsman, and the city dweller, as well as the homesteader.

Drying food is the oldest method of preservation used by mankind and dates all the way back to the so-called caveman era. It was then done by exposure to the sun, not by artificial heat as we do it today. Records exist from biblical days, and long before, of dehydration processes engaged in by the Egyptians, the Persians, Greeks, Hindus, and Chinese. It was a universal and natural way to preserve foods in times of plenty for use in times of famine.

In American colonial times and during the westward

movement, drying food was a daily chore; especially after the autumn harvests, it was an important part of life on the frontier. Dried foods, such as corn, constituted the main source of food for the explorers, trappers, and fur traders, who could not always depend upon killing fresh meat. Dried foods weighed little, lasted long, and contained all the nutrients of fresh products. Without dried food, the French-Canadian *voyageurs* would not have been able to paddle their canoes five thousand miles across the continent and the mountain men of the Rockies would never have survived the winters. Such expeditions as Lewis and Clark's Corps of Discovery could not have succeeded. Quartermaster records show that, in addition to dried corn, beans, peas, and other vegetables, Captain Lewis also purchased a large quantity of "potable soup" in Philadelphia to take along. This was simply a dehydrated soup much like that contained in the instant-soup packets you can buy today in the supermarket.

When I was a lad in North Dakota, my family did not have refrigeration. Neither did anyone else in rural communities. We had an icebox, which in summer was replenished by an ice wagon that made the rounds every day or so with its big blocks of ice cut the previous winter from Downing's Creek and kept buried in sawdust in a barn. Following the ice wagon was a favorite pastime for kids. The iceman would chip off chunks for us to suck on. In winter, of course, anything not kept warm froze solid. Freezing ruined most fruits and vegetables, so in the fall after the harvest, what we could not store fresh in sand or in the root cellar, we dried for winter use.

Today, drying has once again become popular, even with all our modern conveniences and in spite of mechanical refrigeration that is cheap and efficient. As a matter of fact, the latter has led to a new method of food processing — freeze drying — although that is beyond the scope of this book. One of the reasons for the revival of drying is the worldwide interest in "survival" foods for camping,

All of nature's bounty can be easily and inexpensively dried or dehydrated, removing up to seventy per cent of the bulk, but none of the food value or wholesomeness.

fishing, hiking, skiing, and other outdoor pursuits, as well as expeditions away from civilization. The other main reason is economy. A family can store a year or more of food at about half the cost of supermarket shopping — in surprisingly small space and without the need for electricity or refrigeration. Many families, even if they do not rely entirely on dried foods, make use of such foods for 25 or 50 percent of their diet and economize accordingly.

Lastly, and of some concern these days, a well-stocked pantry of dried foods is a hedge against not only inflation but food shortages.

Some Definitions

Before going on, let's settle on some common terms. The Encyclopedia Britannica defines *dehydration* as the process of drying by using an artificial heat source and a fan. If a fan is not used with the heating element, says the encyclopedia, the process is called *evaporation*, not dehydration.

For our purposes we will use "drying" and "dehydrating" interchangeably, meaning the same thing.

We will not be discussing *freeze-drying*, which is a process that removes moisture by convection, in the same way that in the old days the long-handled underwear hanging on the line in freezing weather dried stiff as a board. Modern freeze-drying is a commercial process and not suitable or practical for home use.

As for quality of the product, there is no difference between conventional dehydration and freeze-drying, but the former takes up much less space than the latter.

What do you need in the way of equipment for home drying? You need a minimum size, homemade or factory-built dryer, which can be as small as two feet square. For production or quantity drying, you will of

Mixed vegetables for soup can be dried and stored for later use. Properly stored, the dried product will keep indefinitely without refrigeration.

course need a correspondingly larger unit or maybe two or more units. Some other equipment needed might be:

Deep kettle with close-fitting lid
Perforated rack or trivet to fit kettle
Wire basket, colander, or open mesh bag
Stainless steel knives
Vessels for saline or dipping solutions
Sulfur cabinet
Wood racks or fiberglass screening
Containers for storing dried products: plastic bags, jars, plastic containers, and perhaps a large plastic garbage can with bags for bulk storage of dried foods

What can you dehydrate with your home unit? Just about anything that will fit on the trays, including all fruits and vegetables, and the following:

Herbs   Mushrooms
Fruit "leathers"   Soups
Beef jerky   Eggs
Fish   Shortenings
Yogurt   Milk
Whole wheat cereal   Cottage cheese
Seeds for next year's garden   Granola
Croutons for soup   Potatoes

The unit can also be used for making sourdough starter or raising bread dough.

How can dehydrated foods be reconstituted? Simply by soaking in fresh water, either as is or in the meal preparation process. Caution: Impure water is now a fact of life even in advanced countries such as the United States. A recent government study showed that in eighty major cities, even where water is treated with chlorine and other disinfectants, it is unfit for human consumption. Water filtering kits are available in all sizes, from one that will fit into a coat pocket up to distillers that produce a hundred gallons a day. (See Appendix for one source of home distillers that produce the "pure quill" for drinking, coffee making, and cooking.)

How long will my dehydrated foods keep? No one knows accurately, because conditions vary. Figure on a

four-year shelf life, which is more than double the recommended storage time for canned or "wet-pack" goods.

The four basic food groups — vegetables, fruits,
grains, and dairy or meat products — provide a balanced
diet for good health and resistance to disease. It should
be noted that grains, such as wheat, can be stored indefinitely without drying, if kept in sealed cans with an inert
gas. Home flour mills are also becoming popular for
grinding grains into flour as needed.

Three Basic Conditions

1. You must remove enough moisture to prevent
spoilage. This should be done as quickly as possible but at
a temperature that does not affect the color, flavor, or
texture of the product to any great extent. As much as 50
to 98 percent of the moisture will be removed. For home
units, the lower figure is more likely. It takes a little
practice to get the right balance of heat and breeze. Too
high a temperature or too low a humidity will cause the
moisture to evaporate too quickly — with a resulting
hardening of the outer crust of the food, which prevents
the escape of moisture from the inner cells.

2. The dehydrating process must inactivate or de-
naturalize the enzyme systems in the food. This will be
accomplished if the other conditions are met satisfactor-
ily.

3. Microbial growth can be controlled by the right
conditions, because micro-organisms which grow rapidly
on raw fish and fruits are inhibited by the removal of
moisture.

Some Things To Remember

The best possible products should be selected for drying — fresh and in the peak of condition, firm but ripe in

the case of fruit and vegetables, not wilted or otherwise beginning to deteriorate nor immature. Products that are inferior before drying will be inferior afterwards.

Because enzymatic action takes place quickly in harvested products, there must be as short a time as possible between pickling, preparation, and drying.

To check chemical changes, vegetables should be partially cooked by steaming or scalding; fruits should be steamed, sulfured, or soaked.

While drying there must be thorough air circulation so air can carry away the moisture and be replaced by new air to repeat the process. It may be necessary to stir or shift the products on the racks during drying to ensure adequate circulation. Also, some pieces will dry faster than others and should be removed first.

The heat, either sunshine or electric, should be low to start or the product will sour. Fruits and vegetables lose moisture quickly at first and release it more slowly as the drying process goes on. The main idea is to start the moisture-release process from the *inside* of the product first, gradually working outward.

Conditioning and Storage

You will find that pieces taken off the trays after drying are not uniformly dehydrated. This is probably because they are not exactly the same size, but also because each piece may have a different density or moisture content in the cells. If pieces that are not completely dehydrated are stored with the others, a mold may develop. To ensure uniformity you can do one of two things: Remove only the pieces that are dry and leave the others for a longer period; or remove all the pieces, place them in a cheesecloth bag and continue the drying in air, hanging the bag from a rafter or over a heat register. An alternate to the bag method is to place the pieces loosely

Delicious dried tidbits shown here include dried papaya, apples, pineapple, pears, cherries, and peaches; plus fruit "leathers" shown in jar.

in an open plastic or earthen container and leave uncovered for a week, shaking or stirring the pieces each day.

Some experts recommend pasteurizing the pieces before storing, especially if they have been sulfur-dried. To
do this, preheat the kitchen oven to 175 degrees F. Place
trays of the pieces in the oven. Dried vegetables should
be heated thus for 10 minutes, fruits for 15. Cool before
storing.

For long-term storage, the dried pieces can be kept in
glass jars with tight-fitting lids, in plastic containers, or
in plastic bags. It is best to package the pieces in convenient amounts, such as one would use for one day or one
week. Be sure to label each package with the contents
and the date. After sealing the jars or tying off the plastic
bags, place in brown bags, such as you get from the market, and tie tightly. A year's supply of dried foods can be
stored thus in individual packages placed in a new plastic
garbage can which has been lined with a plastic liner.

All dried foods must be kept from light and heat — and
of course from rodents and insects. Dried products will
keep a minimum of one year thus stored, if properly dried
and cured. Maximum shelf life would probably be about
four years if the pieces were sealed in cans with an inert
gas such as carbon dioxide from a piece of dry ice.

Sulfuring

The home dryer may or may not sulfur the fruit before
dehydration. Sulfuring produces a better quality of product. It will preserve the color, flavor, and vitamin A and
C content of fruit, as well as inhibit insects during the
drying process. Sulfuring is not injurious to health in any
way. The drying process and subsequent cooking eliminate all discernible traces of sulfur.

Here's how:

Peel, core, or pit the fruit and put in a solution of 4
tablespoons of salt to a gallon of water. This will prevent

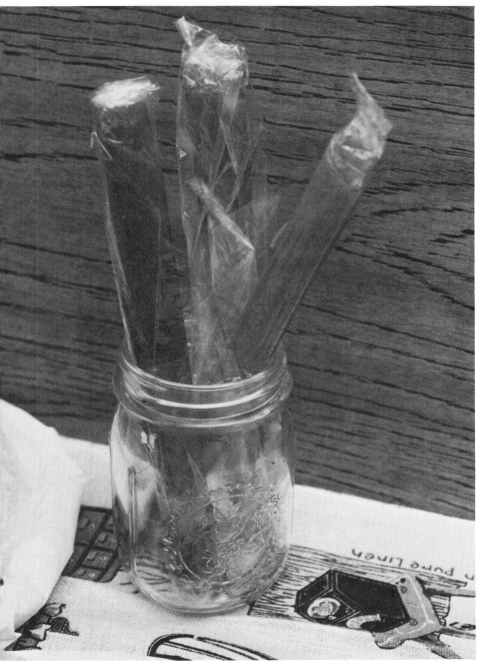

Fruit can be pureed and dried into thin sheets called "leathers," and wrapped in wax paper for later use. They taste like candy, but are unadulterated by sugars or additives. Once kids get used to leathers, they prefer them to store candy.

discoloration. Remove from the solution and drain thoroughly, patting with paper towels until the surface is dry. Now the fruit is ready for sulfuring.

A sulfuring box can be fashioned from a large cardboard box if you do not wish to make a permanent unit. The box should be open on one end; on the other (which will be the top), cut a small hole for fumes to escape. Wooden trays should be used. Place fruit on trays skin-side down. Wooden slats (or fiberglass screening) should be used because sulfur corrodes metal. You will need a shallow pan or metal dish and some bricks. A quantity of sulfur is placed in the metal dish. The trays are stacked above this dish by using the bricks as spacers. The cardboard box is placed over the whole assembly. A small hole is necessary at the top of the box, opposite the open end, and another one near the bottom for ventilation. There should be about two inches of space between the racks and the box sides, and three inches of space at the top and between the sulfur can and the bottom tray. The trays should have a clearance between them of about two inches. The lowest tray should be about eight inches from the ground. Naturally, the sulfuring will be done outside.

Place the fruit on the trays not more than one layer deep, with the skin-side down. The burning time for sulfur will vary with ventilation and weather conditions. If it is free from impurities, it will burn properly. Resublimated flowers of sulfur is recommended and can be purchased from drugstores or chemical houses. Sulfur candles can also be used. Do not use garden dusting sulfur.

Weigh the fruit before placing on trays. For each pound, use 1 teaspoon of sulfur for sulfuring time of less than three hours, 2 teaspoons if the sulfuring time is more than three hours.

First: To light, place the can of sulfur on the ground in front of the lower opening in the cardboard box and light it with a match. Do not leave the matchstick in the can. If the sulfur powder is less than half an inch thick it should burn readily. Try to keep it spread out this way. Place the burning sulfur under the trays. Weight the carboard box so it does not tip over or blow down. Bank a little dirt around the bottom outside edges of the box.

As soon as the sulfur has finished burning, close the ventilation holes and start counting the time. The sulfur dioxide fumes should be given time to permeate the surface of all the fruit on the trays.

Other Methods

1. Sodium bisulfite solution treatment uses a proportion of 1½ to 2 tablespoons of sodium bisulfite to 1 gallon of water. For apricots, soak halves in the solution for 10 to 15 minutes; for pear halves, from 20 to 25 minutes. For peach halves, steam for 5 minutes, then cool to room temperature and soak in solution for 15 to 20 minutes. Sodium bisulfite should be obtainable in drugstores or from chemical supply houses.

2. Ascorbic acid, which is familiar in vitamin C tablets, can be used as an antioxidant, too. It should be available from drugstores or chemical supply houses. It works well with certain fruit. For apples, make a solution of 2½ teaspoons of crystalline ascorbic acid for each cup of water. For apricots, pears, and peaches, the solution should dissolve 1 teaspoon of ascorbic acid for each cup of cold water.

One cup of this solution will treat about 5 quarts of cut fruit. Sprinkle the solution over the fruit as it is being peeled or sliced.

3. A saline dip can also be used. For a solution, dissolve 4 to 6 tablespoons of rock salt to 1 gallon of water. Dip the fruit in this solution.

4. The steaming or blanching process calls for precooking the fruit in steam or boiling water until tender but still firm.

Fruit Preparation

Apples, peaches, apricots, cherries, pears, plums, figs, and all kinds of berries are excellent for drying. Select fruit that is in the peak of condition, ripe but still rather firm. Bananas should be just beginning to turn. The moisture content does not have to be reduced for fruits to the same extent as vegetables.

Use stainless steel knives for cutting or peeling all fruits and vegetables to prevent discoloration. Cut into thin, even slices or into pieces *the same size* for drying, so they can all be removed from the dryer at about the same time. Before placing on trays, prepare the fruits as described above if desired.

Vegetable Preparation

It is very important that only vegetables in perfect condition be used. Wilted ones should be discarded. One piece of vegetable that has started to deteriorate will impart a musty odor to the whole batch.

Sort carefully, discarding any bruised or wilted pieces. Wash the pieces carefully in cold water. Peel or slice according to the particular product method, and then treat or partially cook or steam or scald all vegetables except onions and garlic.

The precooking, steaming, or scalding helps prevent spoilage by killing some of the micro-organisms. It stops certain chemical changes and preserves or sets the color. It checks the ripening process, coagulates soluable molecules, and preserves the vitamin and mineral content. Most important, it breaks down the outer tissue so that moisture escapes from the inner cells more readily.

Steaming is a more satisfactory way of treating vegetables because it preserves the product better without losing any of the nutrients. Use a deep steam kettle with a close-fitting lid and a wire basket. Bring the water to a

Small home dryer is shown with trays loaded with celery, lettuce, and carrots.

boil before putting the basket of vegetables in the kettle. Do not let the water touch the product. Put in a layer of vegetables not over two or three inches thick. Put the lid on and steam until each piece is heated through and thoroughly wilted. To test, remove a piece from the center of the basket and press. It should feel tender. It is better to oversteam than understeam. Remove from steamer and pat the pieces dry with a clean cloth. Spread on trays in the dryer and begin the dehydration process.

To *scald*, remove the wire basket and use more water. Bring to a boil and plunge the vegetables into it briefly. It takes less time than steaming. Test for tenderness as above. Place on trays in dryer immediately.

Sun-Drying

Sun-drying was the ancient's way of dehydrating foods. It was also used on the frontier and is still much used today by farmers and homesteaders. You must have a season of bright sunshine and no rain, so there will be more sun-drying in certain regions and in certain years than in others. The warm, sunny period must come at a time when the fruits and vegetables are ready to pick. The process requires almost constant attention — and protection from insects and rodents with cheescloth or a watchman with a fan. At night the product must be gathered and brought inside and not put out again in the morning until after the dew has dissipated.

For fruit, place pieces on trays one layer deep, place in sun, and turn occasionally. It is best to keep the trays covered with cheesecloth. It will take several days to bring the fruit to a point where it is two-thirds dry. At this time bring trays into the shade and stack. Continue the process until the fruit is done.

For vegetables, after treatment spread in thin layers on trays and place in sun, turning regularly. Leave in sun only two or three days, being careful the direct rays of the sun do not sunburn the vegetables. Complete the drying in open shade.

Oven-Drying

The kitchen oven can be used for drying and for making jerky. The lowest possible heat must be used and the door must be left ajar so the moisture can escape. Most oven doors stand ajar about four inches. Reduce this to about one inch, propping it with something such as a hot mitt. If your oven is so calibrated, set the heat for 150 degrees F. for vegetables and reduce to 140 degrees during the finishing process. For fruits, start at 160 degrees and lower to 150 degrees for the last half of the time. Otherwise, use the lowest possible setting. It will take 4 to 10 hours for vegetables, 6 to 10 hours for fruits. Use an oven thermometer if needed.

Use wooden trays and keep at least two inches between trays. Watch the process regularly and rotate the trays for even drying. Don't forget room temperature and humidity. It may be necessary to open a window or door.

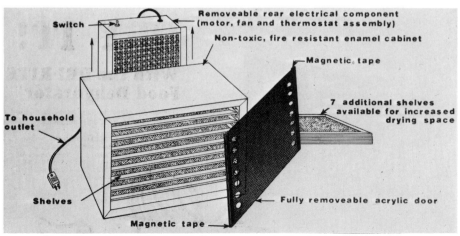

Details of the "Dri-Rite" commercially built home dryer.

Dehydrator Drying

If you purchase a commercially built home dehydrator you will usually find instructions with the unit. If not, or if you build your own, the following general rules can be used. The process is not critical, like pressure canning would be.

1. It is the movement of warm air in the dryer that is the basis for the process. Anything you can do to enhance or encourage this is desirable.

2. The foods should be arranged loosely and in equal sizes and amounts on the trays. If you're using a home-built unit with aluminum window screens, it might be well to cover these with fiberglass screening to keep the food from touching metal.

3. It is temperature control that makes the difference. You need an accurate thermometer or thermostat — or at least one with a constant *rate*. Temperatures should be between 90 and about 105 degrees F., and usually not more than 110 or 115 degrees. Experience will tell you. The higher the temperature, the more you have to watch the product and remove at the critical point. Temperature can be controlled by the thermostat, if the unit has one, or by adjustable vents, usually at the top of the unit.

The food trays should be kept clean. After drying a batch, they should be washed immediately (in the bathtub for ease and convenience). During the drying the trays may have to be rotated, as most units have "hot spots" where drying occurs more quickly. This can be done by changing shelves for trays and at the same time rotating the tray one side at a time (if the trays are square). For drying juicy products such as fruit leathers, use a plastic wrap fastened on the tray with tape. Bakery parchment paper can also be used. Do not cover the entire tray with the paper, as this will inhibit air circulation.

Naturally one should not mix products in the same

batch. Especially do not mix fish or other strong foods with fruits and vegetables. And do not place directly on the screens. Use a piece of plastic wrap underneath (not wax paper).

Fruit Leathers

Leathers are popular these days. Most supermarkets sell them as candy or fruit candy. They usually come in a roll of leathery and chewy sheets. Leathers are made

The simple home dryer developed by Oregon State University is shown here. Plans are available.

from pureed fruit, either fresh or canned. If the latter, it must be drained first. First make the puree. If fresh fruit is used, a preheating step is best to stop the enzyme action. If desired, the puree can be lightly sweetened. Then it is spread thin on a plastic sheet and placed on the dryer trays and dehydrated. When done the leather has a translucent appearance and should be chewy and tasty. When removed from the dryer it should feel dry to the touch, but you can tell better by sampling a piece. Certain types of fruit will feel somewhat tacky, such as cherries and figs.

The leathers can be rolled into sticks with wax paper or can be ground or powdered for use in jellies, recipes, syrups, and soups. They are most commonly used as candylike chewy snacks. Most home dryers mix fruits and nuts for variety in making leathers. An excellent and most often used binder is apple, which mixes well with anything. Try various combinations on your own.

Applesauce leathers made from fresh-picked fruit and pureed in a blender are a treat you have to try to believe. Something about the process seems to concentrate and heighten the delicious flavor of fresh apples.

Leathers can be ground or powdered and mixed into pemmican. They can also be spread with peanut butter for sandwiches. Some leathers, such as pineapple and banana, are indescribably sweet — in fact, too sweet for my personal taste, but children love them. By combining different fruits, any degree of tartness or sweetness can be achieved.

A thing to remember is that the drying process makes all fruits and vegetables seem more concentrated in flavor, especially sweetness, as the process probably brings out the natural sugars and enzyme action more vividly.

All dried products are concentrated, some up to 80 percent. Remember this when using in recipes.

Peanut butter, like apples, can be used in combination

with other foods to make an astonishingly superb leather.

Anything you can puree, as a matter of fact, can be made into leathers. Even leftover chicken and turkey. Mincemeat leathers will convert the most skeptical. And don't forget bread puddings and wet cereals, which also dehydrate nicely into scrumptious munching.

Dehydrating Vegetables

The list of vegetables that can successfully be dried includes but is not limited to:

Beans	Peas	Parsley
Beets	Potatoes	Parsnip
Broccoli	Spinach	Tomatoes
Cabbage	Squash	Turnips
Carrots	Rhubarb	Zucchini
Corn	Cucumbers	Horseradish
Onions	Garlic	Leeks
Mushrooms	Mustard	Kohlrabi

For condensed directions on preparing vegetables and fruits, refer to the chart compiled by the O.S.U. Extension Service. Note that the temperatures used in this chart are considerably higher than recommended for many products. In many cases you will find that 110 degrees F. is more satisfactory. It depends upon your particular dryer, your climate, season of the year, and degree of moisture in the products. Experimentation is the key to success. When learning, keep a record of thermometer readings, time, date, outside weather, and anything else which may have a bearing on the outcome. This is the way to become a true expert.

Vegetables have a shrinking ratio varying from 5 to 1 to 20 to 1, depending upon the type and the degree of dehydration. Watch this carefully so you do not overdry some varieties.

Dehydrated raw vegetables can be reconstituted by

soaking or boiling in water, usually with about five times as much water as the dried product. They can be munched on as is, like candy. They can be ground or powdered in a food mill, added to soups, stews, or sprinkled on salads. The use is limited only by one's ingenuity. Vegetables such as cucumbers and zucchini are excellent for use as chips with dips.

Don't overlook the tops of vegetables such as carrots, which can also be dried and eaten. (*Caution:* Do not eat the tops of rhubarb, which are toxic.)

Tomatoes should be sliced with a sharp knife into ¼-inch slices. Spread out on trays and dry. They can be eaten as is, reconstituted, or made into a powder in the blender or food mill. They can also be cut in wedge-shaped pieces, placed on the trays skin-side down, and dried. They can be chewed as is or added to soups and broths or salads.

Onions should be sliced and placed on plastic wrap on top of trays. dry separately, as the odor will penetrate anything else in the dryer. If dried directly on the screens, you will have a job getting rid of the odor. The green tops of onions, leeks, and garlic become mild and tasty when dried. The sliced bulbs can be used as the fresh product in salads, stews, or sandwiches.

Peppers are very good dried, and can be powdered and used just like condiments you purchase in the store for seasoning.

Rhubarb is usually sliced into ¼-inch cubes and dried as is. It can be used later in pie-filling, alone or in combination with fruits and berries. (Rhubarb is technically a vegetable but is usually used as a fruit.) A delicious cold drink can be made with rhubarb cubes mixed with a little sugar or honey and cold water in a blender.

Green beans and peas can be reconstituted and used as fresh vegetables; they also can be ground or powdered and used in salads, soups, and stews.

Pumpkin can be prepared by first heating the whole in the kitchen oven at 325 degrees for about 30 minutes or

Some of the utensils useful for home drying include food blancher and colander.

so. Then peel and slice or cut into rings. Dry in dehydrator and store. Pumpkin can be reconstituted for pies. The seeds are delicious dried or fried and eaten as nuts.

Zucchini and cucumbers should be sliced about ¼-inch thick, all about the same size for more consistent drying. Use reconstituted or like potato chips with dips.

A *vegetable soup* you will not soon forget can be brewed from powdered vegetables, a little powdered garlic, and powdered herbs of your choice, plus soy sauce and hot seasonings. Perfect for a cold or sloppy day. Also the ingredients can be blended dry, taken on a hiking or camping trip, and reconstituted with boiling water.

Corn can be dried on the cob or, better, shelled first and the kernels dried. The corn silk can be dried as an herb. You will find that corn dried on the cob will taste more like the cob than the kernel. Moreover, the cobs take up too much room on the trays. The kernels can be reconstituted in water and used just like fresh corn on the cob, or powdered in the food mill and used in soups and stews or as corn flour or meal in breads, biscuits, and cereal.

Drying Meat, Fish, and Fowl

Other ways of processing meat, fish, and fowl will be found in the other sections on smoke-curing and pickling, but these products can also be dried or dehydrated in your dryer. Handle only one type of product at a time, especially fish, and keep the pieces as uniform in size as possible.

Jerky is probably the most popular item. Cut good quality, lean beef or venison into ¼-inch strips across the grain. Marinate in soy sauce with garlic and other seasonings for 4 to 5 hours, dry well in the air or pat with towels, sprinkle with black pepper and place on the trays. Dry at the lowest possible heat, testing now and then.

Jerky can be eaten for pick-me-ups like candy, powdered and sprinkled on salads, used in soups, or made into pemmican. Pemmican, by the way, is an old Cree word referring to fat meat and was called such because suet or bear grease was used as a binder. The Indians of Central and South America also made pemmican, calling it *tasajo*. The natives of Africa made it and called it *biltong*.

Chickens, ducks, geese, pheasants, and other birds should be skinned and all of the fatty tissue removed. Cut into thin slices before dehydrating, and use a higher heat. Season before drying. Reconstitute as soups, stews, broths, or casseroles, or powder and sprinkle on salads.

For most *fish*, clean and fillet, removing all skin and fat. Cube into pieces about an inch square, dip in soy sauce, and dry on a plastic sheet until dripping stops. Then dry in dehydrator. Use in chowders, soups, or salads. The product has a distinct flavor, much better than fresh fish.

For small bait fish such as herring, anchovies, or smelt, clean or "gib," slit down the middle, and spread out. Dip in soy sauce. Pat dry and then put into dehydrator for quick drying. The bones can be eaten along with the fish.

The trays will have to be thoroughly cleaned after drying fish. Fish to be stored should be completely dry. To be on the safe side, store under refrigeration.

Drying Berries

Berries are most often made into leathers, probably because some of them are so extremely juicy they are hard to handle otherwise. For leathers they can be combined with apples, bananas, and other "drier" fruits.

Berries should also be dried for other uses. Simply select good ripe, firm berries, clean and spread onto plastic wrap on the trays so they won't drip on the trays below, and dry like anything else. When dehydrated, store or use as powder in pemmican, salads, soups, and stews. They can be reconstituted with water and used as fresh product or on cereals.

Sweetened with honey, they can be spread like jam or cooked with pectin and made into jams or preserves. One of the most delightful products is dried strawberries, first halved and then spread on trays cut-side down. Eat like candy or with cream; use as ice-cream topping or on cereal. Cherries can be dried with or without the pits. Prunes should be pitted first. After drying they can be eaten as is or blended. Grapes dry into really delightful raisins. Currants are excellent dried and have a nice tart flavor. Cranberries are dried as is and reconstituted later for sauce or made into juice, usually blended with apple juice.

Drying Seeds and Grains

The popular granola can be made in the dryer. Here's a recipe: 4 cups oatmeal, ¾ cup sesame seed, sunflower seed, wheat germ, any kind of nuts, coconut, pumpkin seeds, raisins, dates, any dried fruits, bran; plus ¼ cup of honey, ½ cup hot water or enough to dissolve the above; ¼ cup vegetable oil, 1 teaspoon vanilla extract, 1 teaspoon salt. The mixture should be firm but moist. Place on plastic sheet on tray and dry quickly.

Seeds and grains can be dried without any preparation and can be eaten as cereal or without cooking. They can be made into crackers and cookies without cooking by mixing with honey, hot water, a little vanilla, and vegetable oil. Spread out thin and dry like granola.

Any edible seeds, grains, and sprouts can be dehydrated and used by themselves or mixed in combination.

Dehydrating Fruits

Apples are grown the world over and in hundreds of varieties. Johnny Appleseed did his work well in seeing to

Carrots and similar vegetables are best shredded before drying.

this. The culture of apples is a fascinating subject. As a food, apples rank with corn as a universal source of nutrition. Apples are the most versatile of all fruit. You can eat them raw, bake them, cook them into a sauce, make jams, jellies, and preserve with them; make fresh juice and apple cider.

They are also the most versatile of all the products you can dehydrate, not only in their own right but in combination with other fruits and berries. To dry them, peel and slice, or don't peel. Chunk them or shred. The most recommended size, however, is a ¼-inch slice. The pieces should be the same size for uniform drying. Dehydrating takes about two days.

A thin slice of dried apple is just like candy, except that it is healthier for you.

To reconstitute, soak in water, or powder in a food mill and mix with water for apple juice. For applesauce, mix with water and simmer.

Dried pieces of *banana* are the all-time surprise of the year. The taste is completely different from fresh bananas. Cut into uniform slices and place on plastic sheet to prevent sticking to the trays. Bananas should be ripe and even beginning to turn a little for best results, especially if making leathers. Drying takes about two days.

Dried bananas can be made into a delicious dessert or ice cream — blend with honey, vanilla, nuts, vegetable oil, and just enough water to make a thick mix, then freeze.

For just plain eating, slice the bananas lengthwise into sticks before drying.

I've saved the finest treat of all for last: dried *pineapple*. Pineapple has always been my favorite fruit; on a couple of occasions, when seriously ill, my first request has been for pineapple. Apparently this fruit has the necessary vitamins, minerals, and enzymes my metabolism needs. Anyway, it is full of delicious natural fruit sugar, which is the best kind.

Spreading the shredded carrots on the trays for drying. The shreds should be spread out thin enough so that air circulates thoroughly.

Nowadays you can buy fresh pineapple in most supermarkets. Look for ones that are turning a golden color and are getting soft to the touch when pressed. Try pulling out one of the leaves; if it comes easily, then it is ready for eating. Scrub the pineapple on the outside, removing all the leaves or green tops. Cut into four slices the long way. Next, without cutting into the outer case make slices crosswise and lengthwise, so that you have bite-size chunks, like cutting fudge.

Place on plastic paper on the trays and allow plenty of room around each quarter, with the outer case down of course. When removed from the dryer, slice away the chunks from the shell and discard the latter. Eat chunks as snacks like candy, for dessert, for making ice cream, for cereals, or for blending with other fruits.

No matter how you use it, dehydrated pineapple will send you into paroxysms of ecstasy.

Apricots, like bananas, are rich in potassium, which is mandatory for some people with medical problems such as high blood pressure and restricted salt diets. The salt-potassium balance in the human body has a direct bearing on one's well-being.

Apricots can be dried without sulfuring, but they turn dark. This has nothing to do with food value or taste, but many people prefer a lighter color. The apricot seed can also be dried and has an almond taste, but some experts warn that it may be toxic.

To prepare, slice into halves and remove seed, then slice into quarters. Dry until hard, so as to be sure all the moisture is removed. Storage of apricots is somewhat more critical than many other fruits, so follow storage instructions given elsewhere.

---

*Editor's Note: Co-op home economist Betsy Wood comments that "anyone eating apricot kernels should do so at his or her own risk. They contain amygdalin, a substance which releases cyanide in the body. Many people have consumed a few kernels without apparent symptoms but cases of severe poisoning have resulted in California when adults consumed 15 to 48 kernels at a time. Documentation of these cases can be obtained from the California State Department of Health."

To reconstitute, soak overnight in water. Then eat as is or stew, make into leathers, or use in combination with other fruits in jellies, jams, or purees. Sweeten with a little honey, if you like.

Peaches should be peeled or defuzzed with a towel, then steamed or sulfured before drying. Cut into ¼-inch slices, after removing pits, and place on plastic sheet on trays.

Eat as they come from the dryer, or soak and reconstitute for desserts, ice cream, or ice milk; eat with cream and a little honey for sweetening. Make into leathers, or combine with apples or other fruit.

Figs can be dried whole as they come from the tree, without blanching, and reconstituted with water or eaten as is.

Pears are not usually peeled but washed and quartered, then sliced thin. It is not necessary to core pears. They can be quartered and cored if desired, however. Slices should be about ⅛-inch thick. Use in making leathers, or eat as is, or pureed as "butter."

Pit *plums* and *prunes* and quarter them before drying. Put skin-side down on trays. They can be eaten as is or reconstituted with water, which then becomes a rich juice. Use also in leathers and in puddings.

CONDENSED DIRECTIONS FOR PREPARING AND DRYING FRUITS AND VEGETABLES
Temperature for Drying, 140° to 150° F.

	Selection and Preparation	Method	Treatment Before Drying Time in Minutes	Tests for Dryness (cool a piece before testing)
FRUITS				
Apples	Peel and core. Cut into slices or rings about ⅛ inch thick.	Sulfur	60	Leathery; glove-like section cut in half, no moist area in center.
Pears	Peel, cut in half lengthwise and core. Section or cut into slices about ⅛ inch thick.	Sulfur	60, sliced 120, quartered	Springy feel
Large stone fruits	Peel and slice peaches. Cut in half and pit apricots, nectarines, and large plums and prunes. Fruits dry more rapidly if cut in quarters or sliced.	Steam (may omit) and sulfur	5 to 20 / 60, sliced 120, quartered	Pliable; leathery, a handful of prunes properly dried will fall apart after squeezing.
Berries (except strawberries)	Pick over, wash if necessary.	Steam	½ to 1	Hard; no visible moisture when crushed.
Cherries	Pit only large cherries.	White cherries may be sulfured	10 to 15	Leathery but sticky
Figs	If figs are small or have partly dried on the tree, they may be dried whole without blanching. Otherwise cut in half.	Steam	20	Pliable; leathery; slightly sticky
Grapes. Small Plums. Small Prunes. Small	If dried without blanching, a much longer drying time is required. Only Thompson Seedless or other seedless varieties should be dried.	Blanching or no treatment		Pliable; leathery
VEGETABLES				
Beans: bush varieties such as Refugee and Stringless Green Pod	Remove defective pods. Wash. Remove strings from string varieties. Split pods lengthwise to hasten drying.	Steam or pressure saucepan	15 to 20 / 5	Brittle
Beets	Select small, tender beets of good color and flavor, free from woodiness. Wash; trim the tops but leave the crowns. Steam for 30 to 45 minutes, until cooked through. Cool; trim off the roots and crowns; peel. Cut into shoestring strips or into slices about ⅛ inch thick.	Steam (as suggested)		Tough; leathery
Broccoli	Trim and cut as for serving. Wash. Quarter stalks lengthwise.	Steam	8 to 10	Brittle

	Selection and Preparation	Method	Treatment Before Drying — Time in Minutes	Tests for Dryness (cool a piece before testing)
Cabbage	Remove outer leaves, quarter and core. Cut into shreds about ⅛ inch thick.	Steam	5 to 6 until wilted	Tough to brittle
Carrots	Select crisp, tender carrotts, free from woodiness. Wash. Trim off the roots and tops. Cut into slices or strips about ⅛ inch thick.	Steam	8 to 10	Tough; leathery
Corn (cut)	Select tender, sweet corn. Husk. Steam on cob immediately, 10 or 15 minutes, or until milk is set. Cut from cob.	No further treatment / Steam	30	Dry; brittle / Dry; brittle
Leaves for seasoning: celery, parsley		Wash		Brittle
Onions	Remove outer, discolored layers. Slice.	No treatment		Brittle; light colored
Peas	Select young, tender peas of a sweet variety. Shell.	Steam immediately	10	Hard; wrinkled; shatter when hit with a hammer
Potatoes	Peel, cut into shoestring strips ³/₁₆ inch in cross section, or cut into slices about ⅛ inch thick.	Rinse in cold water; steam	4 to 6	Brittle
Spinach and other greens	Select young, tender leaves. Wash. See that leaves are not wadded when placed on trays. Cut large leaves crosswise into several pieces to facilitate drying.	Steam	4, or until thoroughly wilted	Brittle.
Squash (banana)	Wash, peel, and slice in strips ¼ inch thick.	Steam	6	Tough to brittle
Squash (Hubbard) Pumpkin, yellow	Chop into strips about 1 inch wide. Peel off rind. Scrape off the fiber and seeds. Cut peeled strips crosswise into pieces about ⅛ inch thick.	Steam	until tender	Tough to brittle
Squash (summer) crookneck, scallop, zucchini, etc.	Wash, trim, and cut into ¼ inch slices.	Steam	6	Brittle
Tomatoes for stewing	Select tomatoes of good color. Steam or dip in boiling water to loosen skins. Chill in cold water. Peel. Cut into sections, not over ¾ inch wide. Cut small pear or plum tomatoes in half.	No further treatment or may sulfur	10 to 20	Leathery
Powdered vegetables	For use in soup or puree, powder leafy vegetables after drying by grinding fine in a blender or in an osterizer.			
Soup mixture	Cut vegetables into small pieces; prepare and dry according to directions for each vegetable. Combine and store. Satisfactory combinations may be made from cabbage, carrots, celery, corn, onions, and peas. Rice, dry beans, or split peas, and meat stock are usually added at the time of cooking.			

Courtesy Oregon State University Extension Service

II

HOW TO PICKLE THE GOURMET WAY

WE HAD LAUNCHED the boat at the Forest Service ramp alongside U.S. Highway 101 — the only improved access to Tahkenitch Lake on the south coast of Oregon — and rigged up bass casting rods before leaving the dock. The temperature was in the 30s and the aluminum seats were still slushy with ice. Venus hung low in a clear sky now turning light gray, with streaks of dark clouds moving in from the ocean, passing under the waning quarter moon. The surface of the lake itself, however, lay like a dark shag rug, shadowed by the steep forested coastal mountains that squeezed the lake into a series of twisting arms, penetrating into almost inaccessible timber country.

That's how come it got its name. *Tahkenitch*, in the old Siltcoos Indian dialect, means "waters of many arms."

The lake covers only about 1,500 acres but has a shoreline of several hundred miles. Because most of the adjoining lands are in private timber company ownership and because access is so limited — even by boat — the lake remains today almost the same pristine wilderness as in 1603 when this part of the coast was first sighted through the fog by Sebastian Vizcaino.

At least it seems so this early in the morning, before the scars and graying stumps of the old rain forest (logged off almost a century ago) are outlined in the first light. Today much of the scarring is overgrown with second-growth timber, and the area is maintained as a tree farm — in many places an almost impenetrable tangle of undergrowth, wild flowers and berries, and downed trees mingled with new trees. It is a paradise for black bear, blacktail deer, elk, bobcat, and wildlife of all sorts, including the endangered osprey and the lonely great northern loon.

It was early April, and spring was late. The three of us — Doc Buck, Vince Aleksa, and I — hadn't fished the lake for several years and were almost strangers to it. Doc Buck (Dr. Allan Buck), and Vince, manager of a savings and loan association, are two of the most dedicated anglers I've ever known. They fish together at least once a week — on Wednesday, or "Lord's Day" for the medical and dental profession — all year around. They seldom come home without fish and game of some kind, and none of it goes to waste. In fact, were they not professional men with good incomes, they could easily live off the land — and live like gourmets at that.

It is a privilege for me, whenever in the Coos Bay, Oregon area, to spend some time with them, either fishing or hunting. I never fail to learn something about woodcraft, outdoors cooking, or the techniques of expert angling and hunting.

On this morning, just as it started to get light, we got into the fourteen-foot aluminum skiff, and Doc drove us up the dark lake toward remote Five Mile Arm at twenty miles an hour. At this speed the cold morning air sliced clean through my outer rain and inner down jackets and even through the moleskin shirt and knit turtleneck under that. There is nothing so completely frigid as an open boat going twenty miles an hour on a frosty morning on a lake.

At last, just as the sun burst over the top of the ridge and scattered shafts of light over the dark lake, Doc cut the motor and we coasted up to the shoreline, which was choked with underbrush, lily pads, and tules. With the motor off, the silence screamed. The roar of the ocean surf, far away and over the dunes to the west, could be heard clearly. A loon cried its eerie note in a still-dark cove on the other side. The slip-slap of wavelets drummed on the aluminum skin of the skiff.

We began casting for smallmouth bass, using Twin Shannon weedless spinners, from which we had removed the skirts and other entanglements and had impaled black plastic worms on the hooks. You have to cast up under the overhanging brush, into the shallows only a few inches from the shore. This means you get hung up frequently, but there is no other effective way to get at these wiseacres, who are as wily as they are vicious. Usually they strike the moment the lure hits the water. Occasionally they will follow the lure back to the boat and smash it, but not if the water is real clear, as it was this morning. Once my lure sailed over a branch and hung there momentarily. A bass leaped right out of the water and grabbed it. Then I had fun trying to save both the lure and the bass.

Within a couple of hours we had hooked and released a couple of limits. (What's the use of going to this much trouble so early in the morning for only a half hour or so of fishing?) Then, under a darkening sky and rising wind, I noticed a front moving in from the southwest. It was another in a series of weather systems that had been coming in from the North Pacific for weeks. Our promise of a clear spring day was not to be. In a few minutes the rain had started, and a few minutes later we were all three soaked in spite of our heavy foul-weather gear. We went on casting and catching bass for another hour or so. It then being toward noon, Doc drove the boat across to a small remote cove where the remnants of an old wannigan was tied up behind a log boom.

Quickly we got the gear in under the shelter of the wannigan's overhanging roof. Then Doc and Vince broke out the goodies and spread them on a warped and weathered board.

There was a bottle of Vince's special homemade wild-berry wine, a sourdough French bread loaf made the night before by Doc's wife, Jeannie; a home-canned tin of steelhead in Bordelaise sauce, a quart Thermos jug of steaming hot bouillabaisse made with redtail surf perch fillets and chunks of striped bass, a tin of smoked and canned spring chinook salmon, a jar of home-canned spicy-hot baby beans, put up by Vince's bride, Pat; and the *pièce de résistance* of the day — Doc's special pickled shad in sour cream and onions.

Huddled there under the shelter of the wannigan roof, hair stringing down over my wet face and water dripping inside my collar and down my spine, hands numb with cold, eating with frigid, watersoaked fingers, I thought I had never in my life tasted a more exquisite shore dinner.

Doc makes his pickled shad and onions the night before. The shad comes directly out of his salting barrel — in this case a simple plastic container in which he had put the shad in rock salt months before. (Salted shad will keep forever; and older it is, the better it gets.) Taking it out of the salt, where it has been "cooking" or "pickling" for maybe a year, he cuts the shad fillets into bite-size chunks, first removing all the skin. (The bones have already been "melted" in the brine.) He washes the chunks thoroughly, then mixes them with thin-sliced onion rings and a sour-cream sauce and lets them stand overnight in the refrigerator.

That's all there is to it.

I want to tell you that, whether huddled in a freezing rain in a wannigan on Lake Tahkenitch or at a diplomatic soirée in Washington, you will taste nothing so tantalizing, delicate, and delicious. You will be tempted to make a whole meal of it, instead of being satisfied with it as an hors d'oeuvre or smorgasbord treat.

Maybe this is the time to get squared away on a few confusing terms such as pickling, salting, curing, and the like. The word pickling is frequently used for the process of salting or brining, which is in reality a food preservation and curing method. It is also used to describe fish, meat, fruit, and vegetables that have been put up in vinegar and spices.

I think it is proper, and for our purposes here, to separate the different methods of preparing and preserving fish, game, and domestic foods once and for all and call them by the right terms. For one thing, the confusion could lead the novice into some dangerous practices. Pickling is definitely *not* curing. Pickled foods will quickly spoil, and even become toxic, if not protected by salting or brining or canning or freezing. Salting or brining, on the other hand, if the salinity of the mixture is proper, will keep foods indefinitely, especially fish and meat. It is also a curing process.

So let's talk about pickling in its proper context, which is in processes where a vinegar is used. It is almost impossible to buy these products commercially prepared, which makes pickling an even more desirable treat and it is easily done for home use. Almost any kind of fish can be pickled. As you probably know, herring is the one most often used in the Scandinavian smorgasbords. Other good pickling species include shad, mullet, catfish, salmon, steelhead, carp, eel, lake trout, pike, pickerel, haddock, mackerel, sturgeon, and buffalofish, as well as shellfish such as shrimp, mussels, oysters, and clams.

Domestic meat, as well as wild game, vegetables, and fruits of all kinds, can and should be pickled.

The human animal, long before fire was invented, lived high on the dinosaur without cooking it. Cooking (some aficionados regard this as synonymous with ruining) is a relatively new method of food preparation in mankind's two million years of existence on earth. For centuries fish, meat, plants, and wild fruits were eaten raw, thereby giving the eater the full benefit of all the vitamins, minerals, and enzymes so necessary to life. Even today much meat and fish are still consumed by gourmets as well as native cultures in the raw state — usually, however, marinated, dried, or jerked. Fish, particularly, is much better eaten raw or marinated, which is also a pickling process.

Preservation of fish or meat by pickling is a short-

The wholesome foods that our parents and grandparents enjoyed not too long ago are still possible, even in this computerized, supermarket age. Not only are home-cured, smoked, pickled, dried, and preserved foods more wholesome and tasty, but they are a way to beat inflation and keep the family doing things together.

term thing. How long it will keep depends on many things: local weather, refrigeration, the acetic acid content of the vinegar, and so forth. Also, some species of fish do not keep as long as others. To stop bacterial growth, an acetic acid content of 15 percent is required. Ordinary commercial vinegar contains 5 to 6 precent, which is too strong for ordinary taste. However, as little as a 3 percent solution will retard spoilage for up to a week without refrigeration. If kept cooled at 50 degrees F. or lower, the food can be stored for several months; to be completely safe, a temperature of 35 degrees F. or lower should be used.

The preferred solution for pickling is distilled vinegar, because it has a standard, measurable acetic acid content. Cider and fruit vinegars are undesirable, as their acetic acid content is too variable and unstable. Moreover, the fruit residues often give fish an undesirable taste.

Spices used in pickling should be fresh, preferably. Best results are from fresh, whole spices which have been ground and mixed as needed. In a pinch, however, packaged spices obtained from the supermarket condiment department can be used, even those ready-mixed "pickling spices."

In many recipes and processes described here, the fish or meat will already have been salt-cured or brined before the pickling is done. This will be indicated as clearly as possible to avoid confusion, but many of these homemade and old-time methods merely use a vinegar-base brine and a marinating process. So don't let it throw you.

Ordinary salt herring can be pickled in vinegar, but herring not cured especially for pickling is dark, lacks flavor, and is tough.

To cure herring properly for pickling, cut off the head, trim the thin belly flesh to the vent, and clean thoroughly, removing the dark streak along the backbone. Wash in cold, fresh water and drain on absorbent paper or toweling. Pack the fish loosely in a crock or plastic container and cover with a brine (salt and water) solution testing 80 degrees on a salinometer. This would be in the following proportions: ⅝ cup of salt to 1 quart of water, plus enough vinegar to give it an acidity of 2.5 percent. You will find that if you use an equal amount of water and vinegar it will come to about 2.5 or 3.0 percent.

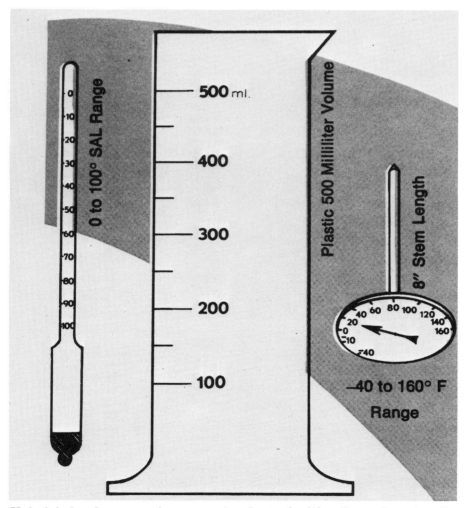

Helpful for home-curing are simple tools like the salometer for measuring salt concentrations in brine, and the dial thermometer.

Leave the herring in this brine until the salt has bled through, but remove it before the skin of the fish begins to wrinkle or lose color. It takes a little practice to give it the proper length of cure to suit your own tastes, but the process is not critical. The length of cure depends upon temperature, freshness of the fish, and the size of the fish. The average time is about five days, more or less. Use five days as a basis to work from.

When cured, the herring should be repacked tightly in the crock, scattering a little dry salt among them. Re-cover with a brine half the strength used first. (The orig-inal brine has been discarded.) Store again in a dark cool place, but *not for more than a couple of weeks.*

The final process in putting up spiced or "pickled" herring calls for soaking the fish in cold, fresh water for at least 8 hours. Remove, drain, and put the herring in a solution of vinegar, salt, and water for 48 hours more. This solution is 6 percent distilled vinegar to 1 gallon of water and 1 pound of salt.

You can skip this last step entirely if you prefer. Many do, using the herring as soon as they have been freshened in water.

Herring Tidbits

Use the following formula for each 10 pounds of pre-pared herring:

1 qt. vinegar	1 oz. black pepper
1 pt. water	1 oz. white pepper
3 oz. allspice	1 oz. red pepper
2 oz. bay leaves	1 oz. sugar
2 oz. mustard seed	½ oz. cloves
½ oz. sliced onions	

The herring is cut into bite-size chunks and packed in layers in a crock or plastic container with sliced onions, bay leaves, and the spices. Cover with vinegar diluted with water, in which the sugar has been dissolved. Let stand for 24 hours in the refrigerator before using. After this you can pack them in mason jars and store for as long as six months at 35 degrees F. or lower. When you put the pieces in the jars, drop in a few whole spices and a bay leaf or two, or perhaps a slice of lemon or lime. Do not use rubber jar rings, as vinegar deteriorates them.

We find these tidbits will not keep six months — or even six days. We eat them up right away.

Rollmops

For this delightful and tasty *pièce de résistance*, first cut the herring into two fillets, instead of chunks, with the backbone removed. Roll each fillet around a small dill pickle and fasten with a toothpick. Stand the rolls on end in a crock, with the following mixture or sauce all around them.

Slowly cook a quart of vinegar with a half pound of sliced onions and one ounce of sugar, until the onions are soft but not mushy. Then add:

1 oz. black pepper	1 oz. mustard seed
1 oz. stick cinnamon	1 oz. bay leaves
1 oz. cracked ginger	1 oz. cloves

Simmer the sauce for 45 minutes but don't boil. Strain out the spices before pouring around the rollmops, after the sauce has cooled. The fish should be entirely covered. Let stand for three days before using. The rollmops will keep about two weeks in warm weather and up to two months in winter at ordinary room temperatures, but it is recommended that they always be stored in the refrigerator — or at least in a root cellar or streamside cooler.

Squarehead Candy

Remove the heads of herring, clean and wash, and drain. Wipe dry and rub belly cavity with fine salt and ground pepper. Place in crock or glass casserole dish with some bay leaves, whole cloves, peppers, and allspice. Partly cover the fish with vinegar and bake in a slow oven until ready to eat (after cooling). These will keep about two weeks without refrigeration.

Siberian Sardines

For each pound of *small* herring or anchovies, make a formula as follows, ground as needed and blended:

1 lb. powdered sugar	½ oz. bay leaves
1 oz. allspice	½ oz. cloves
2 lbs. fine salt	½ oz. ginger
1 oz. pepper	½ oz. hops
½ oz. saltpeter	½ oz. nutmeg

Wash the herring or anchovies. Remove the gills and intestines by pulling them out through the gill flap without tearing the belly or throat. Rinse, drain, and pack in a crock. Cover with 3 parts distilled vinegar and 1 part water. Let stand for 12 hours. Drain, dredge in the spice mixture, pack in crock with bellies up. Scatter more of the spice mixture around and between layers, which are packed crisscross or at right angles to each other. The top layer should have the belly turned down. Cover the top layer with spice mixture. Weight the top layer with a crock lid (no metal) so that as the brine forms it will soak down through.

I prefer to scatter through the layers onion rings, some ground horseradish or sliced capers — not more than ½ pound of onions and ¼ pound of horseradish for 10 pounds of fish.

Cure in the crock for two weeks before using. Fixed this way, the fish will keep several months in a cool, dark place; again, refrigeration is recommended where available.

Pickled Carp

Yes, even the grubby carp can be made appetizing by pickling. First collect the following for the sauce formula:

2 qts. distilled vinegar	1 oz. allspice
2½ pts. water	1 oz. mustard seed
1 oz. red pepper	½ oz. bay leaves
1 oz. white pepper	½ oz. sliced onions

Clean carp thoroughly, remove skin, cut into fillets, and remove backbone. Cut fillets in 2-inch squares. Soak in fresh water for a few minutes, then for an hour in a brine made of 1 cup of salt to 1 gallon of water to get rid of blood and the musky taste. Drain, pack in crock, and cover with a 90-degree brine solution (water saturated with salt until no more will hang in suspension) for 12 hours. Remove, rinse in fresh water, and repack in a crock after scattering some spices on the bottom. Put in a layer of fish, then a layer of sliced onion and spice mixture, then another layer of fish, then a layer of spice formula, and so on. Cover the whole with a solution of 2 parts vinegar and 1 part water, with a small piece of alum.

Boil slowly until fish is soft enough to pierce with a fork. Cook and repack in mason jars with a few fresh spices, a bay leaf or two, a slice of lemon, and several slices of onion. Strain the vinegar sauce and pour over the fish in the jars.

The above recipe can be used with any freshwater fish, including catfish, buffalofish, pike, pickerel, mullet, suckers, or whitefish. For pickerel and pike, I prefer the following:

Minnesota Pickled Pike

Clean and wash fresh-caught pike, pickerel, walleye, or muskie. Cut into fillets, removing the backbone. Make the fillets into short lengths and dredge in fine salt, as much as will cling to the wet fillets. Pack in a crock, leaving about 12 hours. Rinse off the salt and soak for half an hour in fresh water. Cook a mixture of vinegar, water, sugar, garlic, and spices for 10 minutes; add the fish and cook 10 minutes more. Pack the cooked fish in

mason jars that have been scalded, adding chopped onions and some spices, along with a lemon slice in each jar.
Strain the vinegar mixture and bring sauce to a boil. Fill
the jars and seal immediately.

Make the vinegar-spice formula as follows:

1½ pts. water	1 tbsp. mustard seed
1½ pts. vinegar	1 tbsp. allspice
2 cups chopped onion	1 tsp. black pepper
1 clove chopped garlic	1 tsp. cloves
	1 tbsp. bay leaves

Pickled Eels

Eels are hard to come by, but if you can find them
here's how to pickle them. Clean, skin, and cut into small
pieces. Wash well, drain, dredge in fine salt, and let stand
for 1 hour. Rinse the salt with fresh water, wipe dry, and
rub into each piece some garlic from a clove that has been
cut. Brush the pieces with melted butter or salad oil.
Broil until light brown. Place pieces on paper toweling.
When cool, pack them in layers in a crock. On the bottom
and in between layers scatter sliced onion, allspice, bay
leaves, mustard seed, whole cloves, peppers, and mace.
Weight down with a crock lid. After 24 hours cover the
pieces with a 6 percent vinegar-water solution (3 parts
distilled vinegar to 1 part water). Cover crock tightly and
let stand 48 hours before eating.

You won't believe how tasty this can be, even those
who think eating eels is like eating rattlesnakes.

Here's the formula for 10 pounds of eels:

1 qt. vinegar	½ oz. mustard seed
1 pt. water	½ oz cloves
1 oz. allspice	½ oz. black pepper
1 oz. bay leaves	½ oz. mace

Pickled Pacific Salmon

Some people think of salmon only as broiled or smoked

or canned. But pickling best brings out the rich, delicate taste of this premium fish.

For 10 pounds of salmon, you need the following sauce:

1 qt. vinegar	½ tbsp. bay leaves
1 qt. water	½ tbsp. black pepper
½ cup olive oil	1 tbsp. white pepper
1 cup sliced onions	½ tbsp. cloves
1 tbsp. mustard seed	

Cut salmon into small portions, washing well in fresh water. Drain on toweling and dredge in fine salt. Let stand for half an hour, rinse off salt, and simmer fish until done. Don't overcook! Place pieces while still warm in a crock, cover with vinegar-spice sauce made of ingredients above and prepared the following way:

Cook the onions in olive oil until they are soft and yellow. Add the other ingredients and simmer slowly for 45 minutes. Let cool and pour over fish in crock until all pieces are covered. Let stand for 24 hours before eating.

I use this same method for steelhead (a seagoing rainbow trout — best prepared this way instead of broiling or baking) as well as for albacore tuna, mackerel, shad, striped bass, sablefish or black cod, lingcod, sea bass (rockfish), surf perch, and many other kinds of saltwater fish.

Escabeche

In Spanish, *por favor*, this merely means pickled fish. It is a favorite in Central and South American countries. It originated with the Romans, however, when they were big all around the Mediterranean. In Spain it is the most popular method of preserving fish. There are many variations of this ancient recipe, but most of them are based on this formula:

1 qt. vinegar	1 tbsp. red pepper
1 tbsp. black pepper	½ tbsp. cumin seed
2 tbsp. bay leaves	½ tbsp. marjoram
1 clove minced garlic	1 large onion sliced
1 pt. olive oil	

To prepare 10 pounds of fish, cut into serving pieces, wash and drain, and put into a 90 degree brine solution (salt and water saturated) for a half hour. Wipe dry. Pour the olive oil into a frying pan with a clove of minced garlic, half a dozen bay leaves, and a few red peppers. Cook until light brown, put aside to cool. Add onions to the oil and cook until yellow. Add whole black peppers, cumin seed, marjoram, and vinegar. Cook slowly for 15 to 30 minutes. Let cool. Next add the rest of the bay leaves and red peppers and pack into mason jars which have been scalded. Fill the jars with the vinegar sauce and close tightly. Let stand a day before eating. But take my word for it, the longer it stands the better it gets. It will keep about 3 weeks in summer, longer if stored in a cool place. Keep under refrigeration if possible.

Seviche

Seviche is another South American delicacy, but more marinated than strictly pickled. It is sold commercially in the southeastern part of the United States and in the Latin quarter of many large cities. It is really just cubed raw fish marinated in a sour-orange juice. Properly prepared, it is exquisite. But you have to use the juice of the sour orange, a very special variety grown in southern Florida and in subtropical countries. It is *not* the juice of an unripe orange. Good lime juice can also be used, but never use lemon juice. It doesn't work with this formula.

The fish must be fresh-caught and not wormy. As with escabeche, you can use striped bass, corvina, sea trout or weakfish, mackerel, tuna, marlin, sailfish, and even some species of shark.

The ingredients include:

10 lbs. fish	5 cups lime or sour-orange juice
5 large onions	12 to 15 yellow chili peppers
3 cloves garlic	Salt and cayenne to taste

Scale and clean fish, then fillet and remove backbone.

Cut fillets into half-inch cubes. Wash and drain. Slice onions thin, mix with garlic which has been ground fine. In a large bowl mix fish with the garlic-onion mix and season with salt to taste. Slice peppers and add, then stir a little cayenne pepper into the juice and pour over the whole. Sometimes tartaric acid, dissolved in water, is used instead of lime juice. Let the seviche stand overnight before eating. It will keep for about five days at room temperature and much longer if refrigerated.

You can also make seviche with clams, mussels, shrimps, and freshwater crayfish. Prepare the shellfish the same way, but remove the beard from the mussels and the dark body mass from the clams. The insides should also be removed from freshwater crayfish (crawdads), as these are bitter as all get-out.

Gravlax

This was a favorite of my Swedish ancestors, although they used Atlantic salmon while I use Pacific. It is a marinated product served in smorgasbord.

Clean and wash 10 pounds of salmon. (Steelhead can also be used.) Split lengthwise, remove the backbone. Rinse the fillets and dry. Rub oil into both sides. Mix together salt, pepper, ground allspice, saltpeter, and mace, and dredge both sides of the fillets, rubbing well into the flesh. Place chopped dillweed on top of halves, place haves together, and tie tightly with string. Set in casserole dish with a glass lid pressing down on fish for 48 hours. Keep glass jars in refrigerator. Here's the list of ingredients:

10 pounds salmon	¼ cup dillweed or fresh chopped dill
or steelhead	1 tbsp. allspice
1 pt. olive oil	1 tbsp. white pepper
1 cup salt	1 tbsp. saltpeter
1 cup brown sugar	1 tbsp. mace

How To Pickle Shellfish

Most folks like clams, oysters, and mussels fresh, steamed, or fried. But they also are delicious when pickled. The most work is in the cleaning. Scrub the shells well. Steam just enough to open the shells, saving the liquor or nectar, as it is sometimes called. (I just call it clam juice.) Remove the meat from the shells; cool the meat and nectar separately. Pack the meat in scalded mason jars with some bay leaves, whole cloves, and one slice of lemon per jar.

Strain the juice from the steaming process and to each quart add ½ pint distilled vinegar, ½ tablespoon *each* of allspice, cloves, and red peppers, and a teaspoon of cracked whole mace. Simmer for 45 minutes. When cool, pour into the jars and seal. Store in a cool, dark place or in the refrigerator. Be sure it's dark. (If you're quick enough, you may catch that little guy turning off the light when you shut the fridge door). Pickled shellfish, if exposed to light, become light struck easily and turn dark.

Pickled Shrimp

Pickled shrimp is a favorite on the Gulf Coast and West Coast, where there are shrimp industries and the fresh product is readily available. Peel the green fresh shrimp, washing well. Make a cooking brine as follows:

1 gal. fresh water	½ cup salt
1 pt. vinegar	1 tbsp. red pepper
1 tbsp. white pepper	½ tbsp. cloves
½ tbsp. allspice	½ tbsp. mustard seed
6 bay leaves	¼ tsp. mace

Simmer this slowly for half an hour, then bring to a boil and add the shrimp. Cook the shrimp for 5 minutes in a rolling boil. You may have to wait a moment as you add the shrimp, as the cold shellfish tends to lower the temperature. Remove, cool, and pack in scalded mason jars with a smattering of fresh spices and a slice of lemon. Fill the jars with a solution in the following proportions:

2 pts. water	1 pt. 6 percent white, distilled vinegar
1 tbsp. sugar	1 tsp. dillweed

Seal jars tightly and store in a cool, dark place or in the refrigerator.

As one might expect, since there are large colonies of Finns, Swedes, Norwegians, and Eastern Europeans in the seaport town of Astoria, Oregon, it is a place to go for seafood and seafood recipes of all kinds. One of the most famous places is Ocean Foods, a wholesale and retail establishment, the latter department being run by a gentleman named Larry Morris who spends his off-hours fishing and thinking up better ways to pickle fish.

Here are four of Morris's recipes, including the brining solution he uses:

Salt Brine

Dissolve 1 pound of rock salt in 9 pints of water. Place cleaned fish in chunks or large pieces in a sterilized or scalded stoneware crock. Pour salt brine over fish to cover and weight down with a stoneware lid. Soak in the brine for at least 2 days (but the fish may be left in the brine for months).

Pickled Salt Herring

3 lbs. salt herring	1 large onion
1 large lemon	1 bay leaf, crumbled
2 cups white vinegar	½ cup dry sherry
½ cup sugar	2 tsp. mixed pickling spices

Cut herring (about 3 large ones) into 1-inch pieces. Slice onion and lemon very thin. Soak herring in cold water for 3 to 4 hours; drain, rinse, and pat dry on paper toweling. Bring to a boil in a stainless or enameled pot the vinegar, sugar, spices, and sherry. Reduce heat and simmer for 5 minutes, stirring to dissolve sugar. Set aside to cool.

Put the herring pieces in layers in scalded mason jars. Pour in enough cold pickling liquid to cover fish. Let stand in the refrigerator for 48 hours or more before eating. This will keep about 3 months in the refrigerator but is best eaten without delay — as snacks when desired. Make up a new batch when the old supply is gone.

Morris Pickled Salmon

4 lbs. salt-brined salmon	2 medium onions
2 cups vinegar	1 cup water
½ cup sugar	2 tbsp. brown sugar
3 bay leaves	1 tbsp. whole cloves
1 tbsp. celery seed	1 tbsp. mustard seed

The salmon should be soaked in fresh water overnight, then skinned, boned, and cut into bite-size pieces. Slice the onions thin. Layer the salmon and onions in scalded mason jars. The rest of the ingredients should be brought to a boil in a stainless or enameled pot, then set aside to cool. Pour over salmon to cover. Refrigerate for 48 hours before eating. Will keep up to 3 months refrigerated.

Morris Pickled Shad

4 lbs. salt-brined shad	3 cups vinegar
¾ cup water	2 tbsp. pickling spices
1 tbsp. whole allspice	1 medium onion, chopped coarsely
2 bay leaves, crumbled	1 celery stalk, chopped coarsely
1 tbsp. broken cinnamon	stick

Soak the shad fillets for 4 hours, drain, rinse, and wipe dry. Cut into bite-size chunks and pack in scalded jars. Combine the other ingredients and simmer over a medium heat (don't boil). Reduce heat but continue simmering for 45 minutes. Cool and pour over fish to cover. Refrigerate for 48 hours before eating. Will store up to three months.

Morris Pickled Sturgeon

4 lbs. salt-brined sturgeon   1 qt. white vinegar
¼ cup honey   1 large onion
½ cup pickling spices   2 tbsp. bay leaves
Green and red peppers to taste

Use white or green sturgeon; white is best. Rinse and soak for several hours. Wipe dry and cut into bite-size chunks. Layer into scalded jars and pour the pickling solution over when it has cooled. Store in refrigerator for at least two days before eating.

One of the most plentiful of all North American fishes is the ubiquitous smelt, which is found in various species on both coasts and in some large inland lakes. The grunnion of the California and Oregon beaches, subject of many a snipe-hunt joke, is a smelt. So is the Alaskan eulachon, which has been corrupted to "hooligan."

In the Columbia River the annual arrival of the smelt runs is a delightful break in the early spring doldrums and precedes the spring chinook runs. Smelt will appear in the main river as early as December and spawn in various tributaries such as the Cowlitz, Lewis, and Sandy up through April. The arrival of the smelt run is eagerly anticipated and, tradition has it, spring has not arrived until the smelt have returned to the Sandy — in the same way the swallows come back to Capistrano. Unfortunately, some years the little blueback fishes don't return at all, having skipped the Sandy for as many as twelve years in a row. But that's the problem of the local chamber of commerce. Not much is known about the life-style and habits of smelt except that they will show up somewhere when spawning time comes around.

Smelt are so rich in oil that the Northwest Coast Indians rendered them for cooking and candlemaking. They are naturally delicious when fried, which brings out the richness. However, one is quickly satiated. As the saying goes, the first fried smelt dinner of the season is worth $10; the second, you wouldn't eat if they paid you $10.

To catch smelt for home use, sportsmen with long-handled dip nets stand on the banks of the stream as the hordes pass by on the spawning run. The daily limit is usually about 25 pounds, which at times is possible to get with one dip of the net. Smelt are also available commercially in fish markets during the runs. For home use one can freeze them, smoke them, or put them up for sturgeon and salmon bait.

The best way is to pickle them. Here's a recipe given me by my old fishing buddy, Art Lacey, whose Bomber service station, with its World War II B17 bomber hanging overhead, is located on McLoughlin Boulevard in Milwaukie, Oregon:

Lacey's Pickled Smelt

Brine smelt overnight in a solution of 4 cups of salt to a half gallon of water. Rinse in cold water 5 or 6 times. Cut into bite-size chunks (after gutting). Mix 2 cups white sugar, 4 cups white vinegar, 1 cup pickling spices. Bring to a boil; let cool. Add 1 large onion sliced, and pour over fish chunks which have been layered in a casserole dish. Be sure fish is covered by juice. Let stand in refrigerator for 5 days.

Here's the Cowlitz River method of pickling smelt:

Cowlitz River Smelt

2 lbs. fresh smelt	1½ bay leaves
1¾ cup white vinegar	1 tbsp. pickling spices
¼ cup water	2 small onions, sliced
1½ tsps. salt	Several thin lemon slices
	2 tbsp. sugar

Remove heads and tails from smelt; gut. Dredge in flour and fry in oil until golden brown on both sides. Cut into

Home curing is reward enough in itself, when your pantry shelves are loaded with pickled fish, fruits, vegetables, and meat; with smoked, dried, and kippered delights.

bite-size chunks and pack in scalded jars alternately with onion rings and lemon slices.

Combine vinegar, salt, bay leaves, sugar, and pickling spices and bring to a boil. Cool, pour over the smelt in jars, and seal. Let stand 48 hours before serving. Will keep about 3 to 4 weeks in refrigerator.

One of the little-known North Pacific marine fishes is the sablefish or black cod (*Anoplopoma fimbria*). Its range is from Baja California to the Bering Sea, and it is commonly found only in extreme depths up to 170 fathoms. It grows to a length of about three feet and lives 20 years or longer. It is a prolific spawner, and because of the fine quality of its flesh it has in recent years become the basis for a new commercial fishery (stimulated by the operations of the Japanese and Soviet distant-fishing fleets, which have started to decimate the stocks).

The sablefish or black cod is one of the finest of all smoked fish, and fresh fillets are really hard to find in seafood markets. The flesh has a high oil content, and the liver is high in vitamins A and D like the lingcod — neither of which is a cod.

Smoked black cod, if you can find it, is a true delicacy that gives salmon a run for its money in any gourmet contest.

Perhaps the most prized of all is pickled black cod. This is an epicurean delight that all too few humans have yet to discover, and I hope to open up the exploration a little more. The recipe for pickled black cod is even harder to come by, but I am going to reveal one of the better ones right here:

Stonewall Banks Pickled Sablefish

First get hold of a fresh fish or two from a commercial fisherman. (Most black cod are now caught like crabs, in pots set out in water depths up to several hundred feet.)

Clean and remove head and backbone, cutting fish in half. Dry-salt or brine-cure for 5 to 8 days. The salted fish can then be stored under refrigeration for 6 months or more before pickling.

To dry-salt, put a layer of fine salt on the bottom of a large glass, earthenware, or plastic container. Layer the fish skin-side down (top layer with skin up) with alternate layers of salt; cover well with salt. Hold under refrigeration.

To brine-cure, put fish into saturated brine of about 3 pounds of salt per gallon of water, completely submerging the fish. If necessary weight down with a glass casserole cover.

When ready to pickle, remove the skin. Rinse off the surface salt or brine with fresh water, soaking as long as a day if too salty. This salinity will have to be judged by experience, but I prefer it not too heavily salted. Cut into bite-size or serving-size pieces. The fish can also be cut into strips, which is a handy way to eat them.

Place bites or strips into scalded glass jars and cover with a pickling solution. Cure in the refrigerator for one or two weeks. (Note: This same formula can be used for shad and salmon with superb results, but those species should not be cured for more than three days.)

After curing, the fish pieces are repacked in a pickle solution. This prepickling assures a high acid content and lets the bones become soft. Excess fat and membrane can then be skimmed off before repacking. The acidity of the finished product, as monitored by commercial packers, should be high enough to give a pH reading of 3.5 or less.

Here's the pickling solution used in the formula:

3 qts.	(750 mls.)	water
1 gal.	(1000 mls.)	white vinegar, 5 percent
1 cup	(200 mls. or 27 oz.)	granulated sugar
2½ tbsp.	(50 gms. or 6½ oz.)	salt
4 medium or small	(100 gms.)	white onions, sliced
8 tbsp. by volume	(40 gms.)	mixed pickling spices
1 tsp.	(3.2 gms. or ½ oz.)	dry chopped garlic

For sweet, Swedish-style pickle, use more sugar than the above proportions. For a milder pickle, the red peppers can be removed from the mixed pickling spices. (Crescent brand was used in this formula.) The garlic is also optional, but I like it. One or two mashed garlic segments will do for the dry chopped garlic.

Note that I included the metric measure, not to show off my erudition (which is pretty low on the metric scale) but for the benefit of readers who might want to go into a commercial custom operation. The above quantities are good for about 15 pounds of fish. The proportions are measured out for approximately 2 gallons of pickling solution.

Store this product under refrigeration. It will maintain good quality for up to 6 months, but long storage will tend to soften the fish through enzymatic action.

The Pickled Steelhead

The steelhead, native to the Northwest coast rivers, is an anadromous fish like salmon, shad, and smelt. This means it spends its growing years in the bountiful ocean and comes back to the river of its birth to spawn. Unlike Pacific salmon, the steelhead does not necessarily die after it spawns. It may go to sea and come back several times before it is caught or dies a natural death.

Although the steelhead is a close relative of and resembles the squaretailed Atlantic salmon, it is technically a rainbow trout that has got the wandering urge and gone to sea. There is no biological difference between a beautiful rainbow-hued freshwater rainbow trout and a mint-bright silvery steelhead (except the latter will run 15 to 20 pounds in size, compared to 1 or 2 pounds for the rainbow).

As a matter of fact the steelhead, the rainbow trout, and the six species of Pacific salmon are all related to the Atlantic salmon. Sometime back in the glacial ages, when there was an easy link between the North Pacific and North Atlantic, the family got split up and each member developed its own characteristics. Of course, all God's fishes originally came from the sea, for the sea is the mother womb of all living things on earth. But I'm getting carried away from my original point, which was the steelhead.

The steelhead, like the Atlantic salmon, is a superb game fish, a great fighter on sporting tackle, and greatly prized by anglers everywhere. (The steelhead now has been introduced into fresh and salt waters all over the world and is no longer confined to the North Pacific.) Unlike the salmon, however, the steelhead is a lousy food fish. I don't like it any more than rainbow trout when it is prepared and cooked in conventional ways. I do like it smoked, but I especially like it when it is pickled the secret Bill Roberts way.

I once wrote a column for my newspaper, *The Oregonian*, about this. The resulting mail and telephone response from irate readers who don't like anyone taking potshots at their favorite game fish almost overwhelmed me. I thought about taking an immediate vacation, fly-fishing in Iceland, but since I did not have the time nor the money, I ran another column which revealed the special pickling recipe of my fishing pal, Bill Roberts, a traveling wholesale marine and fishing tackle salesman in Northern California. This calmed down my irate readers and even converted some of them, I believe, to my way of thinking — that the only good, dead steelhead is a pickled (or smoked) steelhead.

Here's Bill Robert's recipe:

Pickled Steelhead

2 lbs. cleaned steelhead	½ tsp. white peppercorns, crushed
1½ tbsp. sugar	Dillweed (not seed)
3 tabsp. salt	½ tsp. saltpeter

Remove backbone of fish, cut into chunks suitable to handle. Mix spices and rub fish with the mixture. Put the pieces in a glass casserole dish, arranged conveniently so that dillweed can be sprinkled all around. Let stand for 2 days in refrigerator. Keep top of fish covered with dillweed. Before serving, cut into thin slices or slivers.

A variation of this recipe is to prepare a solution of white vinegar and water in equal parts, substitute brown sugar for the white sugar, and immerse the chunks of fish in the solution, covering entirely with dillweed. Store in refrigerator for at least 2 days, then remove from solution, and serve by cutting into bite-sized morsels with crackers or chips.

My Swedish ancestors brought to Wisconsin and Minnesota from Norsholm (on the Gota Canal ship route) their own special recipe for spiced pickled herring, which I have also used with salmon, steelhead, and smelt. It's called *Inläggning av kryddsill* in the Old Country.

Holm Country Herring

40 fresh herring	1 tbsp. black pepper, crushed
1 pt. water	3 pts. white vinegar
10 bay leaves	1 lb. salt
1 lb. sugar	1 tbsp. red pepper pods, chopped
1 tbsp. saltpeter	1 tbsp. cloves, crushed
1 tbsp. red sambal	½ tbsp. ginger

Clean the fish and rinse in cold water. Wipe dry with paper and place in suitable container. Pour the water and vinegar over the fish. Let stand overnight or at least 10 hours. Place herring and mixed spices in alternate layers. Weight down with a glass lid or similar. Let stand under refrigeration for 5 to 6 weeks. Unless consumed right away place in sterilized mason jars with fresh pickling juice and a slice of lemon. Keep refrigerated.

Right here is a good time to offer some tips on pickling, especially pickling fish. While other foods are suitable for preparing in many different ways, it is with fish that one can take full advantage of this method. One reason is because in the fish world there are dozens of critters which most of us regard as trash and unworthy of catching, to say nothing of eating. These include buffalofish, bergalls, gar, carp, suckers, roach, chubs, and the like — depending upon what neck of the woods you come from. Some Pacific Northwest types, weaned on salmon, think striped bass is a trash fish!

Pickling will turn even the most horrendous looking and tasting fish into the ultimate in gourmet delight. So I guess you can also regard pickling as a good sportsman-like conservation operation, as it makes use of many so-called trash fish and helps keep their population down so that "real" game fish have a better chance of survival.

My old friend, George Reiger, Washington editor of *National Wildlife*, associate editor of *Field & Stream*, and author of many articles and books on saltwater fishing, likes to tell about a man he found one day on the New Jersey beach catching sea robins with a vengeance. Instead of keeping them or releasing them, the guy would snarl and curse while hacking them to bits with his knife, his face contorted in wild, demented grimaces.

When George asked what was bugging him the man retorted that he loathed those ugly monstrosities.

"Ugly monstrosities!" exclaimed George. "Why, they are all God's creatures, just like you and me and striped bass."

There is, George maintains, no such thing as a scrap fish.

Equipment needed for pickling fish is simple: plastic bucket or container, an earthenware crock or two, glass jars — mason jars or the glass jars that store-bought pickles and other things come in — and a selection of spices. Don't use aluminum pots and pans or other metal containers for brining, as the acetic acid in vinegar corrodes metal and can form toxic residues.

In many parts of the country, such as North Dakota where I was born and raised, and Oregon where I have spent most of my life, all the salt you buy is iodized. This is because there is a deficiency of iodine in the earth itself in those regions, and iodine is needed in the diet to prevent goiter and for other reasons. Iodized salt, however, is not good for pickling or smoking fish. Get rock salt or pure granulated salt such as found in kosher or gourmet sections of the supermarket. Iodized salt, when combined with vinegar, imparts an undesirable taste, in my opinion.

The vinegar should be the clear, distilled kind labeled five per cent acid. Experts are able to make use of cider and wine vinegars to impart a special flavor; however, stick with distilled vinegar at first.

The essence of any pickling is in the spices used. Most supermarkets now have an amazing array of spices; if they don't, try the specialty grocery stores or the wholesale importers. If possible, get the fresh spice and grind it yourself. However, to be practical, when you are starting out you can do very well with prepared pickling spices obtained from the market and already mixed.

Here are some spices you might want to stock up on: peppercorns, mustard seed, dillweed; black, red and white pepper, mace, allspice, bay leaves, cloves, garlic, dried parsley, tarragon, onion salt, and many other exotics. Spice bags, of the kind we use for field cooking of crawdads, can be made out of washed Bull Durham sacks or similar bags. These are filled with a blend or mixture and suspended in the boiling liquid. In some parts of the country they sell these bags commercially as "crab boils."

Fresh onions, well picked over, are desirable. Only fresh fish should be used for pickling, except in a few instances as described in this chapter. It is important to cut away all dark or tainted meat, gristle, loose skin, fins, and thin flesh such as on the belly. Normally, you will want to cut the final product into either slivers or small bite-sized pieces which can be handled with the fingers.

Fish such as salmon, corvina, bass, and so on can be eaten with only light marination and even raw. But the stronger, coarse fish such as suckers, carp, and squawfish must be fully pickled; and it is better to pickle, then remove and rinse, and put into a fresh pickling solution for the final cure to make sure the muskiness is taken out.

It is important to pack rings of onions with the pickled fish, as these are just as delicious as the fish and can be eaten separately. When packing the pickled fish in jars for keeping, shake the jars vigorously before sealing to get all the air bubbles out and to mix the spices better.

III

SMOKE CURING MEAT, FISH, AND GAME

SOME YEARS AGO, I returned from a salmon-fishing trip off the mouth of the Columbia River with a limit of three prime, mint-bright chinooks weighing more than fifty-five pounds total after cleaning.

It was a hot August day; the ice was melting rapidly, and my salmon, then worth at least $1.75 a pound at the supermarket (that was some years ago, all right! At this writing it is selling for $6.00 a pound), was in danger of spoiling. Something had to be done quickly. Our refrigerator and deep freeze were alreay jammed with fish and game. I was exhausted from the long trip and lack of sleep, and the nearest custom cannery was thirty miles away.

That's when I remembered the Little Chief portable home smoker I had obtained for testing some weeks before from Phil Jensen of Luhr Jensen and Sons of Hood River, Oregon. I had not had time to even unpack it. This I hastened to do, and without stopping to read the directions I pitched right in to save those fifty-five pounds of prime chinook. I used an old woodsman's secret recipe I had obtained from Bert Taylor of Coos Bay, Oregon, one of the best fishing guides in the West who was still going strong at 75. He told me he had adapted his recipe years before from an old Indian method, improving it mightily.

Here is Bert Taylor's method:
Cut the salmon into slabs or thick steaks — "steaking" it is called — leaving the skin on. Prepare a mixture of ½ cup of brown sugar and 1 cup of rock salt, or ice cream salt

Equipment and ingredients for a typical home smoking operation. Either barrel or plastic pail can be used for brining.

as it is often called. Pat this mixture dry onto slabs, being sure to cover all the exposed flesh; shake off the excess. Pack the salted slabs or chunks in a large crock and leave for 2 to 4 hours. The actual time is not critical; what is best for your conditions will become obvious by experience. *Use no water*. The salted slabs make their own brine.

When the chunks are suitably cured — not more than 5 hours — remove from crock and rinse in cold, clean, fresh water. Pat dry with paper towels. Place slabs on racks in smoker, skin-side down, and smoke gently for about 12 hours, more or less. Use vine maple, alder, cherry, or apple wood for the fire, or even corn cobs.

The result is what I consider the finest and most delectable smoked salmon I have ever tasted. You will never find any better anywhere, on the market or home smoked. The taste is indescribably scrumptious.

Right here I'd like to tempt you with another little secret. For a rich fish such as Pacific salmon (Atlantic salmon are dry and tasteless in comparison), serve in thin slices or shavings, as they used to do in the European gourmet centers. Use a meat slicer to get them paper thin. Serve with crackers or thin-sliced rye bread.

Phil Jensen's little smoker will hold as much as thirty pounds of fish or game for smoking. I did not try to stuff it full, racking only about ten pounds in a batch. But I ended up with about $200 worth of superb smoked salmon and saved the day. Since smoked fish should be kept under refrigeration, I took most of it to the cannery the next day and had it canned for future use, froze what was left that we couldn't eat right away — and looked forward to the next trip off the Columbia.

I confess that I started this section with Bert Taylor's secret recipe to tempt you and make sure you stay hooked on smoke curing so you will read on.

Smoke curing is an art and a science and also a profitable business for home or downtown. If you take the time to master the subject, even for your own use, you will find that your circle of friends has greatly widened. If you pursue it further as a custom home-smoking enterprise, you will find a large part of the gourmet world beating a path to your smokehouse door.

That's why I am going into considerable detail for the rest of this section; including smoking methods for the outdoorsman, the average homemaker, the custom smoker, and even the commercial enterprise. Even if your efforts don't get beyond the Little Chief stage, you should read carefully the entire section for a better understanding of the whole subject — especially since there are some health and sanitation aspects you should know.

Smoke curing of fish and meat is a process as old as man's use of fires for heating and cooking. The method used today is basically no different from that used by *Homo erectus* who hung slabs of red meat over the fire in his cave to keep the flies off and discovered it improved the taste and keeping qualities.

Smoke curing today is still as much an art (which means the result of experience and intuition) as it is a science. The process has three basic steps: (1) the salting or brining; (2) the drying or dehydrating; and (3) the actual smoking.

Here's an important point to remember: Smoking is *not* cooking. That's why I called this section "Smoke Curing," and not "Smoke Cooking."

It is exactly that: smoke *curing*.

Cooked fish and game will spoil quickly; cured or smoke-dried products, with the moisture removed, will keep longer, depending upon how long it has been smoked, how much brine was used, and the weather.

Cooked fish, for example, will quickly spoil without refrigeration. so will smoked fish. The scientists at the Oregon State University seafood laboratory in Astoria, tell me that no fish — smoked, salted, or pickled — should be kept or stored at more than 38 degrees F., to be sure that botulism organisms will not grow. This is a basic rule you should memorize.

In actual practice, however, dried or salted foods will keep indefinitely without refrigeration. Cold smoked products are good for several weeks. They may develop a slight mold (even in the refrigerator), but this can be removed with a vinegar rub.

Kippered or hot-smoked products must be refrigerated and even then will not keep indefinitely. They can, of course, be quick-frozen or canned for lengthy storage.

Smoked or "jerked" red meat will keep indefinitely without refrigeration — but more on this later.

Smoking is basically *drying*. Smoke only imparts the delicate cured flavor. At the same time, wood smoke contains several aldehydes, including formaldehyde, and acetic acid. These have a mild preserving effect on meat tissue and the gelatin in fish flesh, and tend to harden them.

Salt is used primarily to draw out moisture and inhibit bacterial growth (with spices and sugar to add flavor). A solution of five to eight percent salt will stop bacteria in ordinary cases. Fish and meats can be kept indefinitely if dried and salted down. This was the common method of food preservation for centuries, not only on long ocean voyages but also for home and market. The salt fish product was once the staple of European commerce, and there is still a large local and export market for it. It can be noted that the religious taboos regarding meat, fowl, and fish most often have their basis in the economics of food marketing in the olden days.

Heat and moisture are the two red flags of danger in the handling of any fresh fish or meat.

As for fish, spoilage is rapid. The instant it leaves the water chemical changes begin. These are caused by decay of stomach contents and also by the myriad of enzymes that are present in the muscles, fat, and connecting tissue. The process is called autolysis or self-

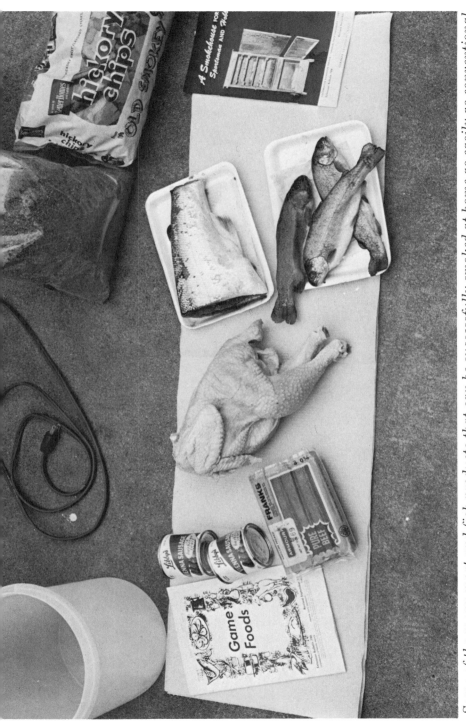

Some of the many meat and fish products that can be successfully smoked at home as easily as conventional cooking.

digestion, and it is this that produces the strong odor and deterioration of flavor. The same thing occurs in picked fruit.

Fish should be cleaned immediately, as soon as landed, and not left in the bottom of the boat or fish box until you get back. Remove the insides and rinse off the blood. If this cannot be done right away, keep fish as dry and cool as possible — don't soak them in water. Pelagic fish such as tuna and marlin are often quick-frozen in the round immediately to stop the decaying process.

Red-meated game and fowl should also be drawn immediately and the body cavity cleaned out, dried, and allowed to cool. This can be done in the field without stopping to skin or pick the carcass. In some cases, such as with venison or domestic beef, the meat is improved by hanging in a cool, dry place to age, but this must be done so that flies or outside contamination are not present.

This aging is sometimes used for certain species of fish. The sturgeon, for example, should be allowed to "relax" for at least forty-eight hours in a cool, dry place even before cleaning. This seems to improve the quality and taste. Incidentally, there is a difference of opinion whether or not the notochord should be removed from the backbone of a sturgeon. This is easily done by first cutting a ring around the small section of the tail, breaking it loose, and then pulling out this long, white sac of milky fluid intact.

If it breaks, they say, it will taint the flesh. Some old Swedes, however, insist on leaving it in, and even pickle it for a delicacy.

Thus the basic purpose of smoke curing is to dehydrate, retard bacterial process, and impart flavor.

A mild smoking can also be used to impart taste to any cooked meat, such as a roast turkey, by first hanging it in the smoker without brining for an hour or so. Packing houses often do this artifically by injecting a smoking fluid with a needle, but this is not recommended for home or custom smoking.

For the commercial, custom, or large-scale smoking of fish and meat, there is a fourth basic: control of heat, or heat "aging." A fifth basic, of little concern to us here, is scientific control of salinity of the brine.

Fish and meat usually must be brined before smoking. The best jerky is also made by first brining the meat — but more about this later. The brine solution is often the most closely guarded family secret of home and custom smokers, guides, and resort operators. With a little practice you too can develop your own secret recipe.

Brining is done by a salt solution, using water or the flesh moisture, or by dry-salting. The type of cure of the finished product is determined by the way it is salted and the strength of the brine. The salt gives the product a flavor, as well as removing the moisture and killing the bacteria. Fish or meat can be lightly or heavily brined, and both methods are called for in recipes that follow. You will remember that in Bert Taylor's method, at the beginning of this section, he used only dry salt patted on.

A *rule:* If the salt solution is under 10 percent, the product should be stored under refrigeration, usually below 38 degrees F. and preferably below 34 degrees F.

After salting or brining, and before smoking, the salt must be removed by rinsing in cold, fresh water. If necessary, scrub the flesh. Then the product must be dried before it is put in the smoker. The length of brining time is not critical, but it does affect the taste and quality of the finished product and must be determined by the individual and his method and equipment. You will note that many methods given in this section have varying brining times. Fish and meat can also be stored in brine without refrigeration until such time as you wish to take them out and pickle or smoke.

In all cases where I have given recipes for smoking, curing, jerking, or pickling, the time given for each step is average or optimum and can, or probably will, vary according to the individual reader.

Note that after brining and rinsing, the fish or meat should be air-dried or patted dry with towels. The more moisture left in, the longer the smoking or drying time. *Humidity control* is very important to custom and commercial smoking operations. Relative humidity, for example, should be below 75 percent. In many parts of the world, the normal humidity of the day is usually higher than this. The Lewis and Clark party, for example, had no trouble smoking and jerking meat on the Great Plains and in the mountains, but in their Fort Clatsop camp at the mouth of the Columbia, where the humidity is high all year, their elk often spoiled before it was cured.

The drying of the fish or meat turns the surface into a glossy, firm sheen, which is called the pellicle. The formation of the pellicle is of great importance, at least in the commercial product.

For the home-style or custom smoker, there are two basic methods: (1) hot smoking or kippering, and (2) cold smoking.

The kippered variety is delicious and best used with dishes calling for smoked products, although it can also be eaten like candy. It will not keep as well as the cold-smoked variety, mainly because it gets some mild cooking in the process.

In my experience, neither variety keeps long in our house — we eat it too fast.

A completely dried and smoked meat, such as jerky, will keep indefinitely. So will a thoroughly dried and salted fish.

Any kind of fish, fowl, or meat (as well as nuts and even fruits and herbs) can be smoke-cured. As far as fish are concerned, the best-tasting are those which have lots of natural oil, sush as salmon, sturgeon, shad, smelt, and herring, but any fish you can eat can be smoked. Bottom species such as cod, sablefish, and sea bass are especially good smoked. Shellfish and crustaceans such as oysters

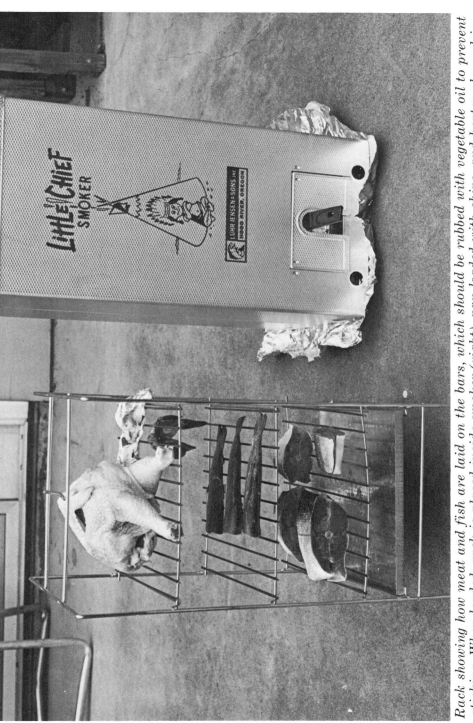

Rack showing how meat and fish are laid on the bars, which should be rubbed with vegetable oil to prevent sticking. When loaded, rack is placed inside smoker (right), pan loaded with chips, and heater plugged in.

are also excellent. The oil content of fish, incidentally, is one of the key factors in the salting process.

Fish products to be canned later should be given only a light smoking, just enough to flavor them. This is my favorite way of keeping smoked fish. I have cans of smoked shad, sturgeon, marlin, yellowtail, swordfish, tuna, and salmon in the pantry at various times. Some species even improve with age in the can. For cocktail parties and holiday open houses, these are usually the hit of the evening.

For smoking fuel, commercial and some custom houses use gas-fired smokers as well as electric ones. The home-smoker can best use either wood, wood chips, or wood sawdust fired directly or heated in a pan by an electric hot plate. The important thing is that the heat source or flames must not touch the flesh or be close enough to it to cause cooking. The Little Chief smoker, for example, has a built-in electric plate on which a pan of sawdust or chips is placed. There are no flames. The heat merely causes the chips to smoke. The heating element is of low wattage, so the smoker never gets hot enough to cook. (On some severely hot days, this could happen, unless the smoking is done in the shade or the cool of the night.)

All types of smokers, of course, use wood (or corncobs) for producing smoke. Any kind of nonresinous wood can be used, depending upon the region. Most evergreens are full of pitch or resin, but I have seen some successful backwoods operations in Alaska and Canada that used fir, spruce, pine, and even hemlock.

In the Pacific Northwest, alder, vine maple, oak, and similar hardwoods are used. An excellent but hard to obtain wood is cherry or apple. I obtain these by hooking up a rented utility trailer and driving a hundred miles or so east to the orchard country. I call personally on small orchards where the trees have been pruned and the limbs stacked for burning. Often the farmer will give me a load just for hauling it away. At home, I cut the wood into convenient lengths or have it shredded in a chipper. The shredded kind is needed for small electric or gas smokers; short whole lengths are used for the open-fire method.

In other parts of the world, hickory, beech, mahogany, birch, and almost any deciduous tree is used. Some custom smokers swear by corncobs as the best of all.

Smokehouses and Smokers

The small, portable home electric smokers, such as the Little Chief, all use a heating element with a metal dish or pan in which you place a quantity of sawdust or chips. There is no flame, and the heating capacity is deliberately limited. If used outside (and certainly they should not be used in enclosed quarters, although a large fireplace can be used) you should be aware of air temperature and wind factor because they affect the length of time needed to complete the process. All smokers should be preheated with smoke before placing the flesh inside.

Most small electric smokers consume about 300 to 600 watts of standard 115-volt A.C. house current at an inside temperature of from 110 to 200 degrees F. A pan of chips will last about 45 minutes to an hour, after which you have to replenish. The smoking can be interrupted and begun again the next day, if necessary, but continuous smoking is best.

Manufacturers recommend that these smokers be set up in the garage with the door open, on the patio, in the backyard, or wherever there is no draft and the temperature is between 50 and 60 degrees F. During the summer you may have to smoke at night, or at least in early morning.

These units are made of aluminum and should be placed on a sheet of aluminum foil. A timing device can be used to control the unit, but I have never found it necessary. In countries where 115 volt A.C. is not available, adapters and converters can be used.

A cheap smoker can be built using an old icebox or refrigerator. Remove all the unwanted insides, including freezer box and crispers. Do not use the rod trays, as they may be coated with cadmium, which is toxic. Drill holes in the top for the smoke to escape and some in the bottom for a fresh-air intake. Use a hotplate for heat, one that has a thermostatic switch. The electric cord can be brought in through a hole or through an existing drain. For a chip pan, use an old skillet or tin plate.

Barrel smokers are easy to build, using an old wood barrel or oil drum with the ends knocked out. Racks or rods for hanging fish are installed at various levels. One version uses a direct wood fire; the barrel is set over it on a brick or concrete base in which there is a fire pit. A small door at the bottom permits tending the fire. A perforated cover is set on top of the barrel; this can be adjusted to regulate the amount of smoke. Small pieces of wood are used for the fire, which must be kept low and almost flameless to prevent cooking. If the fire flares up it can be smothered with a handful of chips or sawdust. Don't use water!

For the best results the firebox should be separate from the smoke chamber and the smoke routed through a duct or stovepipe.

You can even make a usable temporary smoker from a cardboard box. Obtain a large heavy-duty box at least forty inches high and about thirty inches square. Strips of wood can be stapled in the corners or used for battens to hold up the trays. Rods can be wood dowels or iron rods in holes through the sides. Remove the flaps of the box. Use a piece of hardware cloth or fiberglass screening for trays and a sheet of metal or plywood with perforation holes as a cover. Cut a small hole in the side of the box near the top for additional smoke regulation and a larger one near the bottom for tending the fire. Use a hot plate with a pan for chips or sawdust.

Slabs of bacon, purchased in the bulk, can be greatly improved by hanging in smoker for several hours. This is a smoker made from an old refrigerator.

A small open fire can also be used but must be watched closely and smothered with sawdust if it flares up.

With this makeshift smoker, a batch of fish can be processed in about six hours.

For the home craftsman who likes to build, a more efficient smoker can be fabricated easily with wood, hardware cloth, and sheets of aluminum. (Don't use galvanized metal.) Sources of plans are given in the Appendix. These units are about forty-eight inches square and about four or five feet high but can be any convenient size, either portable or permanently installed. They can be of sheet metal, plywood, or a fire resistant pressed hardboard. There is usually a system of adjustable trays as well as holes for hanging rods. The fish or meat is hung from rods or placed upon trays, depending on the type of smoker. Both rods and trays should be adjustable for height or distance above the bottom. Some have sheet metal baffles to direct the smoke, and some are double-insulated for better heat control.

These units are best mounted on brick or concrete bases, with a separate firepit connected by a terra-cotta flue pipe about six inches in diameter. A damper can be installed somewhere in the line for heat and smoke regulation. Usually the entire front of the house is hinged and swings out to give access to the trays and rods.

An existing outdoor fireplace or barbecue pit can be adapted for smoking by fashioning a metal cover with a draft door to fit over the chimney or flue section. A means of controlling the amount of smoke and heat is helpful.

Permanent smokehouses are usually more than four feet square and seven feet tall. Some are even walk-in types and are usually much more elaborate in smoke and temperature control. But some of the crudest log cabin types found in backwoods fishing camps in the North Country produce an excellent product.

The only difference betweeen the permanent and the portable or homemade variety is that the former is larger, handles more fish or meat at one time, and is more sophisticated in the use of controls.

Fort Clatsop, the first U.S. military post west of the Mississippi, was designed around a meat house which was actually a smokehouse. The fort was built in 1805 on a small river near the present Astoria. A large smoke-fire was kept going all the time, as hunters constantly brought in deer and elk to hang. This building can be inspected today in the restored facility. The obvious defect of this smokehouse was that there was no way to control humidity. Also, the wood used was a resinous variety, and there was no brining.

A highly efficient commercial smokehouse has been developed by the Washington State Department of Fisheries (see Appendix and drawings). Many large custom smokers use a similar design, which allows exact control of smoke quality, volume, air flow, temperature, and heat.

Out in the woods or mountains, caught without a portable electric smoker (or an extension cord long enough), you can still smoke your fish or game.

Clean and remove heads of fish. Make a fillet cut above and below the backbone, break backbone but leave tail section intact and uncut. Open fish so it lays flat in one piece. Score flesh lengthwise from head to tail with quarter-inch cuts, about an inch apart. Rub the flesh thoroughly with salt to which a sprinkling of pepper has been added. One ounce of pepper to 1 pound of salt is the proper proportion.) The fish may now be stored in a cool place until ready to smoke. Before smoking, rinse the fish in cold, clean water — usually after hanging all night.

Hang the fillets, after rinsing, to dry in the sunlight, or until the flesh has a glazed appearance.

Meanwhile you will have dug a firepit and got a fire going. When the fire has died to red coals, prop the fish slabs on the forked end of a five-foot length of green limb over the coals. Keep fish well up from the hot coals so they smoke instead of cook. Use green wood to create the smoke, adding more as needed. It will take from five to 16 hours to complete the process.

An inexpensive small smoker and grill for portable use has also been developed by the Washington State Department of Fisheries. This is a combination of smoking and barbecuing, and it imparts a unique but delicious taste and texture to any kind of fish or seafood. Details of construction are shown elsewhere.

Here's how to use it:

Build a hardwood fire and let it die down to red coals. Smooth out the coals and place the grill right on top of them. It can be used for almost any fish, red meat, or fowl; the method is about the same as for salmon, halibut, sole, or cod.

Clean and split the fish, spread open and flat on a piece of aluminum foil. Salt and pepper to taste and baste with a sauce. For salmon use a cup of tomato catsup, 2 tablespoons of Worcestershire sauce, and ½ pound of garlic butter. Mix ingredients thoroughly, spread on top of fish. Cook for about an hour with the lid slightly open, regulating the draft. Watch the process carefully because fish should not be overcooked. When the flesh is flaky to a fork, it is properly done.

Cutting and Hanging

The small home-style smokers usually have simple removable grates upon which meat or fish are placed. The flesh can also be hung by hooks, and often this is preferable, especially with fish and fowl.

Hooks can be fashioned of metal rods in an S-shape. Use stainless rods if possible, but never galvanized or cadmium-plated ones. If the fish are large they can be suspended by a rod through the gills. They should be propped open if not filleted. It is more common to remove heads and split the fish so they lie open and can be placed skin-side down on trays. Sometimes the split fillets, still

The Japanese kamoda will also double as a smoker, or will smoke and cook fish and meat at the same time.

attached to the tails, are simply draped over rods or on a stick. The important thing is not to crowd the smoke chamber and to be sure all parts are equally exposed.

Fowl such as chickens, turkeys, quail, chukars, and pheasants are always hung. I prefer hanging them by the neck, with the body cavity propped open at the bottom.

Brining Methods

One of the more confusing aspects of smoke curing is the brining process. As mentioned before, there are many ways of doing this; often you will find a different brining recommended for each smoking recipe. Don't let it distract you from the main object, which is smoke curing.

You do not have to smoke-cure salted or brined fish or meat; but for best results all fish or meat must be brined or salted *before* smoke curing.

There are sound chemical reasons for brining, and the degree of salinity has been worked out scientifically for custom and commercial operations. Salt tables are given in the Appendix, but the sportsman and home smoker need not be so scientific.

There is a similarity between brine-curing, corning, salt drying, and pickling (vinegar curing). These were the common methods of food preservation for centuries. In this section we are mostly interested in presmoking processes. See the section on Pickling for related methods.

Rather than try to give you one common method of brining for presmoking purposes, I will detail the best or recommended brining method for each step and each of the various recipes and methods that follow.

Salting and Aging

The exception might be in the use of the small home or

portable smokers. These can be used for smoke flavoring, and no brining is required because the meat or fish is then cooked the conventional way. One hour in the smoker will impart all the smoke flavor you will want.

Salting and aging is especially good for smoking game and fish. For a wild game meat, use a mixture of 1 part salt and 1 part sugar, and rub into cut pieces of meat (except for antlered or horned animals). Cut the pieces *with* the grain. After being thoroughly rubbed, the pieces should stand in a cool place for 6 to 8 hours. Rinse with cold water, then drain and dry at room temperature for an hour or so. Hang in smoker with plenty of space around each piece to allow even smoke circulation. Smoke for 12 to 16 hours.

For antlered or horned animals, use the same salt-and-sugar mixture. Cut the meat into pieces about 1 by 3 inches, 8 to 10 inches long. Cut with the grain. Rub with the salt mixture, let stand for 8 to 12 hours. Rinse and drain at room temperature until the meat has a grayish hue — 2 to 3 hours. Hang over wire or on racks and smoke for 16 to 20 hours.

For fish, use the same salt-and-sugar mixture. Clean fish thoroughly and rub mixture inside and out. Pack one on top of another in a clean hardwood barrel or a crock, weight down the pile of fish with a crock cover, and leave for 6 to 8 hours in a cool place, not over 50 degrees F. Then rinse in cold, clean water, drain and dry at room temperature for an hour. Place in smoker for 5 to 8 hours in the case if small fish, 8 to 16 hours for large fish or fillets.

Fowl can be processed with the mixture changed to 2 parts salt and 1 part sugar. Rub inside and out, wrap in damp cloth, and cool for 8 to 10 hours at not over 50 degrees F. Remove the wrapping and rinse in cold, clean water. Drain and dry at room temperature for an hour or until the skin has a dry look. Hang, cavity opening down (for a bird such as a duck, goose, or partridge) using a cord to hold each leg apart and up to the rack center bar. Smoke for 2 hours per pound, then cook in the kitchen oven at 250 degrees for 15 minutes to the pound, or complete cooking on the barbecue rack.

Domestic chicken can be processed the same way but should be smoked for 5 to 8 hours, then put into the oven for 15 minutes at 300 degrees.

Fast Brining

For a faster brining method, prepare a solution in a nonmetallic container. For fowl, mix ½ gallon of water, 1 cup salt, ½ cup sugar, and ¼ ounce pepper. Stir until dissolved. Place cleaned bird in brine and pickle for 1 hour to the pound. Remove and rinse with cold water. Drain and dry at room temperature. Smoke for 1 hour to the pound. Remove and bake at 300 degrees in the kitchen oven for 15 minutes to the pound.

For fish, use a mixture of 1 to 1½ cups salt, ¾ cup sugar, and ¼ ounce pepper to each quart of water. Place fish in brine so that the pieces are completely covered. Brine for 4 to 6 hours. Two or 3 crushed bay leaves can be added to the brine for flavor.

Remove and rinse in cold water and drain at room temperature until the pellicle forms. Smoke for 3 to 4 hours for small fish such as trout. For large fish or fillets, smoke 10 to 16 hours. A little experimenting goes a long way here. For species such as bass, mackerel, or carp (and carp makes one of the finest smoked delights), dip pieces in hot water to remove skins before brining. For oysters, clams, and small pieces of seafood, stretch a layer of cheesecloth on a piece of screening and place on grill racks in the smoker.

To smoke ham, haunches, rolled or fillet loins by this process, use a spiced brine as follows: ½ gallon water, 2 cups salt, 1 cup sugar, 1 teaspoon ground cloves, and 1 cup cider vinegar. Using a nonmetallic container, bring the brine mixture to a boil. Place meat in brine and boil for 5 minutes to the pound. Remove and rinse with cold water

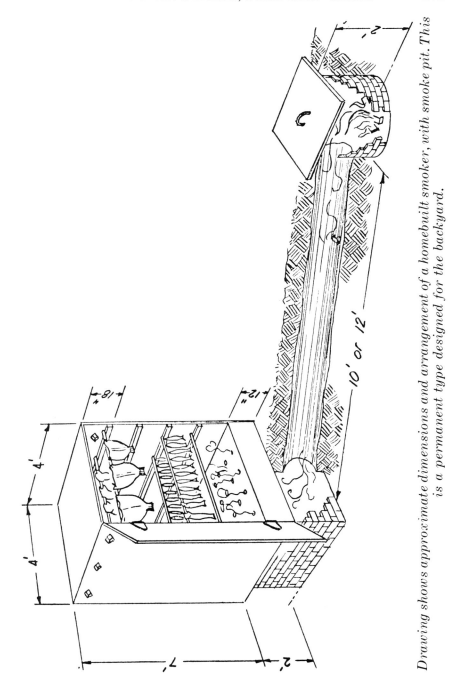

Drawing shows approximate dimensions and arrangement of a homebuilt smoker, with smoke pit. This is a permanent type designed for the backyard.

and drain at room temperature for one hour or longer. Truss with cord and hang on crossbar of rack. Smoke for 1½ hours per pound.

Rabbits can also be processed in this way, hanging 4 at a time in the smoker.

For heart and tongue, use a mixture of ⅓ cup sugar, ¾ cup salt, 1 teaspoon crushed black pepper, and enough water to cover the meat. Boil for 40 minutes to the pound. Drain dry. Rub with garlic clove. Smoke for 15 hours, remove and chill. Serve thin-sliced.

Hot Smoking or Kippering

To elaborate more on this: The fish are held closer to the heat source with this method. They are cured at temperatures of 150 to 200 degrees and are partially cooked. This improves the taste, but the product does not keep as long. Fish most commonly kippered are herring, shad, trout, and salmon, although any fish can be used. In general, this is the way to do it if you plan to use the product right away without cooking:

Fillet the fish or split along the backbone so that it will lay flat, making cuts under the backbone. Wash thoroughly and soak in a 70-degree brine (see tables) or about ½ cup of salt to a quart of water for 30 minutes to leach out the blood.

For a brine, try a mixture of 2 pounds salt, 1 pound sugar, 1 ounce saltpeter, 1 ounce crushed black pepper, and 1 ounce crushed bay leaves in a 90-degree brine solution. If more mixture is needed, increase by the same proportions. The spices can be used according to personal preference. Hold fish in this solution anywhere from 2 to 4 hours, depending on the size of the chunks or the degree of cure wanted.

Remove and rinse in fresh water, hang up to cool, and dry for a couple of hours or until the skin gets shiny as the pellicle forms. Then place in smoker, which meanwhile has been preheated.

During the first 6 to 8 hours (less time is needed for the small electric smokers), keep the fire low and let the temperature build up slowly. After this heavy smoking, increase the temperature to between 130 and 150 degrees F. and let cure for 2 or 3 hours, or until the surface has a nice brown look and seems done.

Remove from smoker and let cool for a couple of hours. If desired, the chunks can be brushed while warm with a vegetable oil to improve appearance and give a protective coating. Melted paraffin is also used to coat kippered chunks, but this is usually done only if the fish is not to be eaten immediately. The wax must be removed before eating. Each piece should be wrapped separately and kept in the refrigerator.

Cold Smoking

In cold smoking, the fish are hung farther from the heat source and cured over less dense smoke at temperatures of 90 degrees F. or less. The degree of preservation depends directly upon the length of smoking time. As long as a week or 10 days is often needed. For smoking meats and fowl, the same general method is used.

Small species such as herring are usually smoked in the round (that is, without gutting) but should be "gibbed." This is the name for making a small cut just below the gills and then pulling out the gills, to which are attached the heart, liver, and intestines, leaving the belly uncut. If the fish is more than a pound in size, split open along the backbone, leaving the belly uncut, and remove all blood, black skin, and viscera. Clean especially well under the backbone. If the head is cut off, leave the bony collar below the gills to support the hook when the fish is hung.

Next dredge each fish in salt, as much salt as will cling

to it, and pack in even layers in an earthen crock or wooden box. Sprinkle salt between the layers. Leave for up to 12 hours, depending on the moisture of the fish, the weather, size of fish, and amount of curing wanted.

Species such as herring, mackerel, salmon, or halibut may be kept thus for up to a year without refrigeration, but the longer in the salt, the less the quality of the smoked product.

After removing from the salt cure, wash thoroughly in cold, fresh water, scrubbing off all loose parts or hard particles of salt. Hang up to dry out of the sun — in the shade and breeze if possible. Use an electric fan, otherwise. In about three hours the pellicle will be formed, and the fish can now be hung in the smoker.

A low smoldering fire should be started, or the electric smoker preheated, an hour before hanging the fish. For the first few hours the smoke should be light — 8 to 12 hours for a 24-hour product, 24 hours for a longer product. The temperature should be no higher than 90 degrees in the warmer climates such as Southern California or the South. In northern latitudes and the Pacific Northwest, 70 degrees is recommended. Use a thermometer, if necessary, to get this heat right. If none is available, test with your hand thrust in where the fish are hanging. If it feels warm, the temperature is too high.

After the initial light smoking, the smoke should then be built up to a dense smolder for the rest of the time. As a rule of thumb, fish to be kept for up to two weeks should be smoked 24 hours; for a longer time, 1 to 5 days is best. For small species such as herring, 2 or 4 weeks is often used.

For cold smoking, the process should be continuous, without interuption.

In the case of salmon, steelhead, and trout, a variation of the cold-smoking process greatly improves the taste and quality. Clean and remove the heads and backbones, splitting the fish into two slabs. Wash these pieces thoroughly, removing all ragged pieces and blood. (Blood hardens and discolors the flesh.) Place the slabs in a 90-degree brine (see tables) and chill with ice. Keep in brine for 1 or 2 hours, then remove and drain for 15 minutes or so. In a crock or wooden box, prepare a salting mixture as follows:

2 lbs. salt	1 oz. crushed bay leaves
1 lb. brown sugar	1 oz. crushed allspice
1 oz. saltpeter	1 oz. crushed cloves
1 oz. white pepper	1 oz. crushed mace

(Enough for 20 pounds)

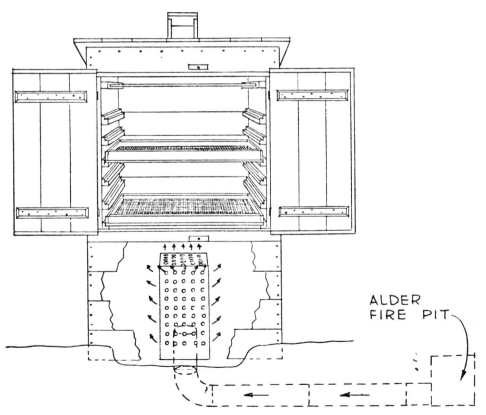

ALDER
FIRE PIT

Another sketch of permanent type backyard smoker which anyone can build for a few dollars and some scrap lumber.

Place fish in box, one slab at a time, dredging the mixture into the flesh and using as much curing mixture as will cling. Cover with a loose lid and weight down. After 8 to 12 hours, remove and thoroughly rinse all traces of salt. Hang the slabs to dry for 4 to 6 hours, using a fan if necessary. Place in smokehouse under a mild heat of not more than 100 degrees F. for 6 to 8 hours. Then build up a dense smoke and continue for another 16 to 24 hours at a temperature of not over 70 degrees F. If a longer preservation time is desired, continue the dense smoking for up to 2 days.

Remove from smokehouse and cool for several hours. Brush with vegetable oil and store in a cool, dry place.

For white-meated fish which are large enough to produce fillets of at least a pound, clean and cut into fillets, removing skin and backbone. Cover with a 90-degree brine and soak for 2 hours. Cure over a heat source for 4 hours at a low temperature of not over 90 degrees F. and a light-density smoke. Turn over and smoke for another 4 hours. Smother the fire with green wood or intensify the smoke and hold until flesh is a deep straw color, turning if necessary. The last phase of this process should take 4 to 6 hours. Cool and wrap the chunks separately in wax paper and store in a cool place.

Custom Smoking

Commercial and custom smoking and canning operations are regulated by state and federal food and sanitation laws. In addition, for good uniform results a more controlled process is used. Careful handling of the product, before and after, and proper sanitation of facilities are of utmost importance. Brine solutions and degree of heat and density of smoke must be positively controlled. The commercial unit, described elsewhere in this section, is one that is built to meet all these criteria. For use with such commercial units, here are some formulas:

For commercial sale, the chinook, "white king," or chum salmon are considered best. They are usually custom kippered. Any species of salmon or trout can be used, however.

The fish is cleaned and cut into fillets, usually a whole side in size but often in about 1 pound pieces for marketing convenience. Soak the fillets for ½ to 3 hours in 90 to 95-degree salinity brine. The time will depend on the size of the pieces and the amount of salt flavoring wanted. This is best determined by making small batches; it could be up to 8 hours in some cases. Remove the pieces from the brine and rinse in cold clean water, draining thoroughly.

If for resale, dip the pieces in a solution of coloring. The solution is a dye approved by the Federal Food and Drug Administration. The one commonly used by commercial houses is "150 orange I," an aniline dye. A solution of about 3 to 4 ounces of dye per 20 gallons of water is average, but the degree of color can be changed by using a different proportion. The dye is made by mixing the concentrate first in a small amount of warm water, then adding the balance of the water. Each piece is dipped about 15 seconds.

Rub the screens on the trays with a vegetable oil to prevent the fish from sticking. Cottonseed, soya, or corn oil is commonly used. Place the fillets so that each is separated from the others. The smaller pieces should be kept separate because they will have to be removed first, as they require a shorter smoking time.

Preheat the smokehouse unit to 100 degrees F. Place the racks inside, then let them dry for an hour or longer, using the blower with both intake and exhaust dampers open. Close the dampers to the half position and start smoking, maintaining the same 100 degree temperature for another hour. Raise the temperature slowly to about 170 degrees F. or slightly higher and continue smoking another hour. Inspect the pieces at this time and remove the small, thin ones if they are done. Continue smoking the rest of the fillets for 1 more hour, then bypass the smoke and open the dampers full. Allow the fish to cool to outside temperature before removing. Wrap immediately and store in a cool place. This product is perishable, although it can be kept frozen for months.

Smoked and Canned Fish

Custom shops do a lot of this because there is a ready market and the product brings a high price. It also enables one to handle a large and sudden surplus of prime fresh fish. Fish stored in the freezer is often brought out and handled this way also.

If frozen, the fish should be thawed slowly by immersing in running water. Either fresh or frozen, fish that are smoked before canning seem to have a richer, more flavorful quality. It is definitely a gourmet product and is usually put up in small cans with fancy labels. Some species, such as shad and sturgeon, are not only much better smoked and canned but also seem to improve with age. In the case of shad, the process softens the bones, which are otherwise a great nuisance.

Fish to be canned after smoking should be given a mild or "light" smoking. Oversmoking is undesirable.

After a light smoking, the product is canned immediately in conventional metal cans or vacuum-sealed jars. If cans are used they can be sealed with a vacuum closing machine or by steam exhausting and sealing. (For canning techniques see references in Appendix.)

Fish to be smoked and canned are not filleted but are cut in chunks of a thickness to fit the cans. Remove the backbone from each piece, but do not remove the skin at this time. Wash the pieces under a fresh water spray and drain. Soak the pieces in a 95-degree salinometer brine for 2 hours. Drain and rinse under the spray. Let stand for 15 minutes.

Place the pieces skin-side down on the screens and put

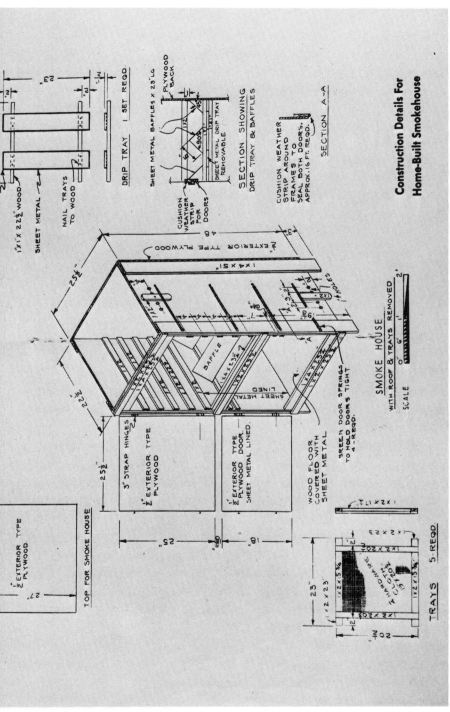

Details for constructing a home smokehouse. Smoke source can be an electric hotplate, or an open pit fire with smoke piped to smokehouse underground. (Courtesy O.S.U.)

trays in the smoker. Turn the fan on and dry for a half hour. Then start the smoke and continue for 3 hours or so, meanwhile gradually raising the temperature to 170 degrees F. Inspect for the proper pellicle and, if need be, continue smoking for 2½ hours. The last phase of this process imparts the smoked flavor and crisps the fish so that the skin can easily be removed. Cool and pack the pieces solidly in the cans. If half-pound cans are used, add an ounce of vegetable oil. Vacuum seal or steam exhaust and seal. Process at 10 pounds pressure for 75 minutes at 240 degrees F.

Smoked and Canned Shellfish

Oysters, clams, and other types of seafood can also be custom processed this way. For oysters, use only the live product and wash the shells thoroughly to remove sand and dirt. Steam for 5 minutes in pressure cooker or retort or 15 minutes in a steam box. This is better than shucking the usual way because it improves the texture and flavor. Remove meat from shells and wash. Soak for 5 minutes in a 60-degree brine.

If the oysters are large, cut in half before brining. Rinse and drain. Place the meat on the screens, put the racks in the smoker, and preheat to 110 degrees F. Smoke for 1 hour with dampers fully open. Close dampers and smoke about another half hour, raising the temperature gradually. Smoke an additional half hour. Exhaust smoker and cool to room temperature.

Pack oysters in quarter-pound cans or flats, adding 1 ounce of vegetable oil to each can. Vacuum seal or steam exhaust and seal. Cook for 60 minutes at 240 degrees F. and 10 pounds pressure.

For clams, open and steam for a short time in a steam box. Remove the meat and clean by splitting open the neck and cleaning out the stomach. Wash thoroughly in fresh water. Divide the clam into neck, foot, and mantle sections. Soak in a 60-degree brine for 5 minutes. Rinse, drain, and place on oiled screens. Preheat the smoker to 105 degrees F. and smoke for half an hour with dampers full open. Then close the air intake, adjust the exhaust, and smoke for 2½ hours with a gradual increase of temperature to 140 degrees F. during the last half hour. Exhaust and cool to room temperature. Use half-pound tuna flats with 1½ ounces of vegetable oil in each. Process at 240 degrees F. and 10 pounds pressure for 75 minutes.

Smoked and Canned Small Fish

Smelt, anchovies, herring, and similar bait-sized fish can be processed successfully as a gourmet product. The most important thing is to use strictly fresh fish as soon as possible out of the water. For anchovies, remove the head and guts and wash in a diluted salt solution, about 3 percent, to remove any blood and loose scales. Drain for a short time, then put in a 60-degree brine for 10 to 15 minutes. Place on screens under a water spray and wash. Drain and place on oiled mesh and put trays in smokehouse that has been preheated to 110 degrees F. Dry for about an hour, then smoke for 2 hours, while raising the temperature gradually to 150 degrees F. Cool to room temperature, pack in half-pound tuna cans or quarter flat cans. If using the tuna flats, put 1 ounce of vegetable oil into the can before packing. Place fish in alternate rows, head to tail, back side down. Add another half ounce of oil. Vacuum seal or steam exhaust for 10 to 15 minutes. Seal and process for 75 minutes at 10 pounds pressure at 240 degrees F. Cool with water immediately.

Smelt are processed the same way, except they should be brined for 45 minutes in a 60-degree solution. If the heads are left on they may be hung from rods; otherwise place on oiled trays. Dry for 3 hours at 110 degrees F. with dampers open. Then adjust the dampers to one-third open and start the smoke, gradually raising the temperature to between 130 degrees and 140 degrees F. Continue smoking for up to 8 hours. Exhaust smoke and cool to room temperature.

The smelt may be eaten as is, stored under refrigeration, or canned. The color comes out a fine golden brown, and there is enough natural oil to keep the fish moist.

Herring are smoked the same way, but the end product is dry, without the natural oil of smelts.

Cold Smoked Salmon

This is the commercial or custom way of processing for the "candy market" — fresh off the counters. A mild cured or hard salted salmon is used. These are obtained from fish packers or can be cured yourself. Soak the fillets in fresh running water for up to 24 hours, depending on thickness. Dress and remove loose particles. Drain by "water horsing." This means stacking the fish, skin-side up and weighted down to force the water out. When drained, place on oiled screens or hang on hooks. If the fish is to be consumed immediately or quick frozen, give only a light cure. For the longest keeping time, increase cure to suit.

For a light cure, maintain temperature at 85 degrees F. with the blower on and dampers open and dry for 3 to 4 hours. Close intake damper, adjust the exhaust, and start the smoke. Continue smoking for 8 to 10 hours, not getting the temperature over 85 degrees F.

For a heavy cure, handle the same as the light cure, except dry for 2 hours at 85 degrees F., then smoke at the same temperature for 5 to 6 days with both dampers about one-third open, adjusting to suit. Refrigeration is not necessary for short periods, but do not attempt to store at less than 38 degrees F., especially during the warm months.

Note: In these commercial and custom operations, the

Another view of a homebuilt smokehouse, developed by Oregon State University. The smoke pit underneath can be fired with a hotplate, or any source of heat as long as it is not an open flame.

reference to a "60-degree brine solution" does not mean *temperature*, but the salinity measured on the salinometer.

Flavor Smoking

One of the benefits of smoke curing food is that the smoke imparts a delicious, tantalizing flavor to meat, fish, cheese, and even nuts. The homemaker can achieve this flavor in many cases where it is not necessary or practical to go through the entire smoking process. A smoke flavor can be added to many foods before roasting, baking, or broiling by simply placing them on the racks in the smoker for about an hour or so. Remove and cook or bake in the usual way. The smoker should be preheated to the proper temperature before starting.

Foods processed this way can also be enhanced by first marinating or brushing with smoking or pickling spices.

Frozen Fish and Meat

In some cases, frozen fish and meat products are equal to or even better than fresh for smoke curing. It depends on the product and how it was frozen. In all cases, frozen products should be thawed at room temperature before placing in smoker.

Proper freezing of surplus fish calls for first removing the fins, tail, head, and undesirable flesh or skin. If a large fish, cut into chunks or fillets. Prepare a solution of 1 cup salt to 3 quarts water and dip the fillets or chunks in this. Place fish in empty milk cartons, plastic bags, or suitable containers and fill the remaining space with cold, fresh water. Leave room for expansion when frozen.

Fish can also be frozen by first double-wrapping in moisture-proof paper. Then seal in an air-tight container to prevent oxidation or freezer burn.

Thawing at room temperature is usually best, but in warm or humid periods, thaw by placing in refrigerator at about 40 degrees F. for several hours. Fish can also be thawed under running tap water, provided your tap water does not have a chlorine taste.

Fish should not be kept frozen more than six months to retain the good qualities. It is then time to remove and smoke or can or prepare fresh for the table.

Here's a tip for judging the condition of fish: Press gently on the skin of the fish with a finger. If the skin springs back into its original shape again, it is fresh; if the indentation remains, be careful — spoilage has already set in. Another good test is the nose. If the fish smells strong, it's deteriorating. In fact, if it smells, it may already be too late.

The Old-Time Arts

Although commercial and custom smoking operations are well standardized, the art of home smoke curing is as varied as the individual. The best way to handle this, I believe, is to include here a sort of potpourri of as many of the old-time methods as space permits, each a complete recipe in itself for the reader to experiment with or alter to suit.

Kippered Salmon

One of the most popular home methods for kippered salmon and steelhead is as follows:

Halve the fish lengthwise or cut into chunks. Soak in a brine solution with the proportions of 20 ounces of salt to a half gallon of water. The flesh should be completely covered. Soak for 2 hours. Remove, drain, and dry for an hour or so at room temperature. Smoke lightly for 6 to 12 hours. When a nice pellicle has formed, hot-smoke or barbecue for 2 hours, with a heavy smoke and a temperature of about 180 degrees F., which partially cooks the fish.

Sugared and Spiced Salmon

For sugared and spiced sides of smoked steelhead or salmon, place in the kitchen in the above brine solution and chill with ice to make sides firmer and stop the oil from oozing. Drain for 20 minutes. Then fill a separate container with the following:

2 lbs. salt	1 oz. crushed bay leaves
1 lb. brown sugar	1 oz. crushed allspice
1 oz. saltpeter	1 oz. crushed cloves
1 oz. white pepper	1 oz. crushed mace

Rub mixture lightly into fish and keep in pan for 10 hours. Remove and rinse, scrubbing to eliminate all the salt mixture. Dry in air for 6 hours. Smoke over a light heat for 8 hours. Build up a dense smoke and continue smoking for 20 hours at about 70 degrees F. If a longer-lasting product is wanted, smoke for another 24 hours. Cool and brush with vegetable oil.

Indian Candy

Indian or hard-cured salmon or steelhead is a popular appetizer. Small salmon such as coho or sockeye are used for this. Brine overnight in a solution of 40 ounces of salt to 1 gallon of water.

After brining, fix whole sides on sticks, or suspend strips with a cord. Dry for 24 hours or blot dry with paper towels. Smoke with a good draft and light smoke for 2 weeks at low temperature. This product keeps well — up to two or three years under ordinary refrigeration. If a surface mold appears, scub with brine and smoke for another 24 hours.

Sugar-cured Rainbows

Rainbow trout are delicious when sugar-cured. Split and open fish. Rub each with a handful of salt then a handful of brown sugar. Place in layers in wooden barrel or crock, skin-side down. Sprinkle each layer with black peppercorns. The top layer should be skin-side up. Place in a cool spot overnight. Then wash in cool, fresh water for 20 minutes. Stack and press out moisture. Blot dry with towels. Smoke for 2 to 3 hours at about 85 degrees F. until a nice pellicle is formed. Smoke another hour at 110 degrees F., then an hour at 120 degrees F., and longer if necessary.

Cosmopolitan Smoked Fish
For this delicacy, make the following solution:

1 qt. water	¼ oz. pepper
1½ cups salt	3 crushed bay leaves
	¾ cup sugar

Soak fish in this solution for 4 to 6 hours. Light smoke for 8 to 20 hours at 85 degrees F.

Nestucca Smoked Salmon
An old fishing buddy from down Nestucca River way in Oregon uses this recipe:

Soak salmon chunks in brine for 6 hours or so. If you are using frozen salmon, soak only 1½ hours. Remove from brine and wipe dry. Place in a cool place to air dry until the pellicle or glaze forms. This takes about half an hour. Then place chunks in smoker for up to 10 hours.

To make the brine for this recipe:

2 cups plain salt	½ gal. water
½ tsp. garlic powder	1 lb. brown sugar
½ tsp. Wright's Liquid Smoke	½ tsp. coarse pepper
½ tsp. Johnny's Seasoning	3 tbsp. molasses

Indian Style Fish
Cut a medium size salmon into suitable chunks of about 4 to 5 pounds each — sliced crosswise, not filleted. To make the brine, mix 1 gallon boiling water and 4 pounds table salt. Cool. Put salmon in a crock or plastic

container and cover with brine. Use a plate or weight to hold salmon under liquid. Let stand 24 hours in a cool place. Remove, wipe dry, and wrap as follows:

Wrap wax paper around the chunks. Next wrap a sheet of white butcher paper around this. Then wrap two thicknesses of moist newspaper around the packages. Finally wrap the packages with four or five layers of dry newspapers and place on alder coals.

Leave the wrapped fish on the coals for 15 to 20 minutes, turning frequently so that all sides cook and until all paper is burned except the last layer of wax paper, which also comes out charred. Peel paper and skin from fish chunks and serve hot or cold.

Dan's Sure-Fire Flavor Cure

This is the flavor mix another fishing buddy uses in his curing brine for both smoked fish and jerky:

White pepper	Allspice
Onion salt	Ginger
Garlic	Lemon juice
Molasses	Dillweed
Honey	Mace
Brown sugar	Bay leaves
Maple flavoring	Tabasco sauce
	Soy sauce

The exact proportions used, he won't even reveal to his bride (after all, you can always get another wife). The enterprising experimenter, however, will have no trouble concocting his own special mixture using the above ingredients — and possibly some substitutions.

Smoked Shellfish

Crayfish, prawns, lobster, crabs are all delicious when smoked. If they are uncooked, do so in the usual way and shuck the meat. If not already cooked, you can also precook in a bouillon for 4 or 5 minutes. In any case, brine the meat in a standard fish brine for 2 hours. Rinse under tap water and dry on paper towels. Arrange on oiled screen or cheesecloth which has been oiled with vegetable oil and place on smoker racks. Arrange pieces of meat or shrimp so they do not touch each other. Smoke for 1½ hours.

Smoked Oysters

Scrub oysters under running water with a brush. Shuck with a knife or steam open. Oysters can also be opened by placing near the coals of a barbecue bed for a few minutes or until they smile at you. At this time you can eat them as is — or better yet, smoke 'em.

After removing from shells, blanch the oyster meat by placing in a strainer and dipping in boiling water until the edges curl. Rinse with cool water.

Put oysters in the standard fish brine for 45 minutes or so. Remove and air-dry for an hour. Then put oysters on an oiled screen or cheesecloth on the smoker rack and smoke for an hour. You have to watch oysters closely to see that they are not oversmoked. You can tell when they are done because the edges dry out.

Smoked Clams

Clams can be opened the same way as oysters. Remove the meat and split neck. Cut out stomach with scissors. Wash in cold water. Remove any sand or unwanted particles. Cure in standard seafood brine for half an hour. Remove and air-dry for an hour. Place on oiled screen in smoker for 2 to 3 hours.

Smoked Herring Or Anchovies

Clean fish by removing head and guts. Large fish can be filleted, if desired, by splitting down the back with a sharp knife. Brine in the standard seafood mixture for half an hour. Remove, rinse, and air-dry. Smoke for 2 to 3 hours. The dry cure method of brining can also be used and the time increased to 6 hours or so.

Smoked Quickies

1 lb. fish fillets	⅛ tsp. paprika
2 tbsp. butter or oil	Onion rings
1 tsp. Worcestershire	Lemon juice

In a greased baking dish place fillets and onion rings. Sprinkle with lemon and Worcestershire, salt, pepper, and paprika. Place in smoker for 1½ hours. Remove and place uncovered in kitchen oven for 20 minutes at 350 degrees F.

Smoking Small Game Birds

This method is good for ducks, grouse, quail, ptarmigan, pheasant, chukar, and even domestic chicken. Until you've tasted smoked bird, you haven't really tasted good fowl.

The birds can be smoked fresh, or frozen ones can be used if thawed completely.

Prepare the following brine in a crock or nonmetallic container:

½ cup brown sugar	1 cup curing salt
4 tbsp. black pepper	1 tbsp. onion powder
1 bay leaf	¼ cup lemon juice

¼ tsp. maple flavor

Mix brine thoroughly. Submerge birds, which have been halved or quartered, in the brine and hold down with a plate. Cure for 1 hour per pound of bird. Remove and rinse under cold water. Wipe excess moisture an air-dry for an hour. Before placing the birds in the smoker, rub the following mixture into the meat:

½ cup brown sugar	1 tbsp. onion or garlic powder

4 tbsp. black pepper

Smoke the birds for 1½ hour per pound of meat. Brush the outside of the meat every hour with butter or a butter sauce — or teriyaki, barbecue sauce, or even beer.

It is impossible to give exact times for a job like this. The best method is to test the bird from time to time. Do this by twisting the leg bone. If it moves freely in the socket, the bird is ready to eat. If your smoker is outside and it is a cool day, the inside of the birds may not be completely done. In this case, remove to the oven indoors and finish off at 300 degrees, but be careful not to over-cook.

Smoking Large Birds

Large birds mean turkeys or geese. There is no known way to smoke an ostrich. A 10 to 15 pound turkey, how-ever, fits nicely into one of those portable aluminum home smokers, and the result is superb.

First make the brine:

4 qts. water	1½ cups curing salt
½ cup brown sugar	3 cups cider
½ tsp. ginger	4 tbsp. black pepper
½ cup lemon juice	½ oz. maple flavor

If more brine is needed, the same proportions should be used. Mix thoroughly in a nonmetallic container in which the entire bird can be submerged. Simmer over a medium heat for 5 minutes per pound. Remove bird from brine and air-dry for an hour. Rub skin with brown sugar. Place bird in smoker, which has been preheated, and smoke for 1 hour per pound. Every hour, baste bird with melted better or sauce.

Remove bird from smoker and finish off in the kitchen oven at 300 degrees. The bird should then have a rich golden brown color with free-moving joints.

Hot Smoked Pheasant Or Duck

Birds should not be skinned. Brine whole bird for 12 to

24 hours in a solution of 1 pound salt, ½ pound brown sugar, and ½ ounce of black pepper for each gallon of water. Remove from brine, rinse in cold fresh water, and air-dry. If desired, you can at this time rub into birds a flavoring such as garlic powder or Tabasco. Place in smoker for 4 to 6 hours, basting once an hour with melted butter or a sauce. Finish off in the oven at 300 degrees with door ajar. Best served cold.

Smoked Tongue or Heart

1 tongue or heart of beef or venison   ¾ cup salt
⅓ cup sugar   1 tsp. black pepper

Place in cooker and add enough water to cover meat. Boil for 40 minutes per pound of meat. Drain and dry. Rub garlic clove or sauce into meat. Smoke for 15 hours. Remove and chill before serving.

Hams, Haunches, Loins

Prepare a brine of:

½ gal. water   2 cups salt
1 cup sugar   1 tsp. cloves ground
            1 cup cider

Make enough brine to cover meat, using these proportions. Place brine and meat in suitable container and bring to a boil. Boil for 5 minutes to the pound. Remove and rinse meat in cold water. Let stand for 1 hour or more. Place in smoker for 1¼ hours per pound.

This same formula is superb for smoking whole rabbits.

Glazed Smoked Ham

You can greatly improve the taste and quality of commercial ham and bacon. Score meat with crisscross

A meat slicer is recommended for thin-slicing smoked products such as salmon and bacon. The secret of superb smoked salmon, in fact, is thin slices, instead of chunks.

slashes. Rub into the ham or bacon slab the following mixture:

1 cup brown sugar	Cloves
1 cup curing salt	Pepper

Place meat in smoker and smoke for 3 hours. Brush meat with a solution of the spice mixture diluted with water. Smoke another hour and remove and cool.

The same delightful hickory flavor can also be imparted to store-bought pork roasts, frankfurters, pork steak, spareribs, pork chops, pork hocks, and Canadian bacon in the same way, with or without the spice rub and before cooking.

Smoked Bean-Hole Beans

Prepare a bean pot or casserole and smoke for 3 hours or so in the smoker, stirring occasionally. Remove pot from smoker and bake in a preheated 350 degree oven for 1 hour. Note: If starting from scratch with dried beans, you have to go through the usual soaking preparation before preparing the beanpot.

Smoked Cheese

Jack and swiss cheese are delicious when smoked, with a tangy sharp flavor that cannot be duplicated any other way. Place cheese in baking dish or cup and place in smoker for 1½ hours. Remove and cool, then refrigerate.

Sweet Pickle Brine

This is a special brine that usually can be obtained from commercial butcher supply houses. If not, it can be prepared at home. It is ideal for curing hams, loins, small cuts of meat and wild game, and bacon. Use the following proportions:

1 gal. water	1 lb. salt
1 tsp. saltpeter	1 clove crushed garlic
	1 oz. pickling spices

The correct salinometer reading should be 60 degrees (see Appendix). Prepare spices by boiling in a small amount of water. Add to brine. To pickle meat, keep immersed in a crock in a cool place, if possible around 40 degrees F. air temperature. If the salt content is not high enough or the air temperature is above 40 degrees, there is some danger of spoilage. If there is a decided change in color of the brine, or if you smell something sour, destroy meat and sterilize crock immediately.

This brine is especially good for wild game and for tough cuts of beef; it will make a delectable tidbit out of the poorest. This solution can also be injected into large pieces of meat with a brine pump, obtainable at a butcher supply house.

Smoked Salt

Try this sometime and see if it doesn't add a new dimension to your dinner table. Place ordinary table salt in a shallow aluminum pan and smoke for 3 hours or until it turns an amber color. Remove and fill a spare saltcellar with it.

Smoked Garlic Bread

Mix equal amounts of butter and sharp process cheese. Add enough garlic powder to suit your taste. Cut a loaf of sourdough French bread into thick slices but do not cut all the way through the loaf — leave the slices attached by the bottom crust. Spread the cheese, butter, and garlic mix into the cuts, covering the slices thorougly. Wrap loaf in aluminum foil. Heat in oven for half an hour at 250 degrees F. Open foil and place loaf in smoker for 30 minutes. Remove and serve warm.

Smoked Nuts

Use a sheet of aluminum foil perforated with many holes. (A fork is a good tool for this.) Place foil on smoker racks. Spread nuts over foil — any kind of nuts from peanuts to chestnuts. Smoke lightly for 2 hours. Nuts, like cheese, should not be smoked too much.

Seeds can be smoked the same way, except that after they come out of the smoker put them in the kitchen oven at 300 degrees F. for an hour, with the door ajar. A variation is to first soak the seeds overnight in a brine solution such as used for jerky.

Smoked Berries

Huckleberries, blueberries, serviceberries, choke-cherries, or almost any kind of wild berry can also be smoke-dried in a smoker. Spread them out on a fine screen or cheesecloth and cold-smoke until they are dehydrated. Keep in a covered container such as a mason jar. When desired, serve on breakfast food or in a bowl with cream and sugar. Dry-smoked berries will keep indefinitely. They are also ideal for making pemmican.

Smoked Eggs

Hard boil a dozen eggs, then store in the fiber or plastic carton they came in until ready to use. Many housewives don't know how to boil eggs. Here's how: Fill pot with enough cold water to cover the eggs completely. Add 1 tablespoon of vinegar. Start the heat and bring to a boil from a cold start. Remove pan from heat immediately and let eggs cool slowly. When cool to the touch, break end and peel.

To smoke, place boiled eggs on screen or cheesecloth on smoker rack and smoke until they turn a golden brown color. If desired, sprinkle with a seasoning mix. Serve sliced, or in a salad dressing, or deviled.

Cans of home-cured and packed salmon, shad and sturgeon. Many prefer the cans to glass jars, but the cost is higher and can stock is becoming difficult to obtain in small quantities. Glass jars are just as good and easier to use.

Corned Beef Cure or Pickle Mix

Two-week pickle:

1 gal. water	3 lbs. salt
½ oz. saltpeter	½ oz. white sugar

Four-week pickle:

1 gal. water	2½ lbs. salt
¼ oz. saltpeter	¼ oz. white sugar

Use a large crock or glass container. Beef brisket or rump is ideal for this pickle cure, as are tongue or shoulder. Remove all bones and cut meat into 3 or 4 pound chunks and pierce with a sharp knife or icepick. Keep pickling container in a cool place between 35 and 40 degrees F. The pickling mixture tastes best the second time it is used, but you've got to start someplace! When meat is removed from pickle, wipe dry and wrap in freezer paper. It can be frozen for later use or smoked.

Many old-timers spike their pickle brine with a cheesecloth bag filled with onions, celery, carrots, bay leaves, mustard seed, allspice, and garlic.

You be the judge.

RECIPES FOR USING SMOKED FOODS

Broiled Smoked Fish

Freshen smoked fish in cold water for 1 hour or longer. The time depends on the degree to which the fish has been salted. Drain, dry, and sprinkle with cooking oil or butter. Preheat broiler to 350 degrees F. Place fish on racks, skin-side down. Broil 3 minutes on each side. Serve with lemon or melted butter.

Baked Smoked Fish

Freshen as above and dry. Place on a greased baking pan or dish, skin-side down. Brush with oil and sprinkle finely diced carrots and onion on top. Cover with milk. Bake 20 minutes to 1 hour, depending on size of slab and degree of smoke. Baste with milk as it evaporates. Remove and garnish on platter.

Smoked Fish In Milk

Freshen 2 or 3 pounds of smoked fish. Drain, dry, and place skin-side down on a greased pan or skillet. Pour a cup of whole milk or cream over the fish and dab with 3 tablespoons of butter or cooking oil. Sprinkle with salt and pepper to taste. Cook slowly in the oven or over a slow fire for about 10 minutes. Remove and garnish with cooking liquid and parsley.

Creamed Smoked Fish

1½ cups cooked flaked fish	4 tbsp. oil
1 cup milk	1 tsp. Worcestershire
1 cup fish stock	Salt and pepper to taste
4 tbsp. flour	

Make a white sauce of flour, oil or fat, salt and pepper, and fish stock. Add Worcestershire. Stir smooth and add fish flakes. Heat thoroughly. Serve on toast, rice, or hot biscuits. The recipe can be varied with the addition of peas, boiled egg, carrots, or green peppers.

Smoked Fish Patties

2 cups ground fish	½ cup milk or cream
2 cups cracker crumbs	Pepper to taste
1 egg	

Beat the egg and add the other ingredients. Knead

into patties. Melt butter or heat cooking oil in skillet and fry a golden brown.

Smoked Fish Soufflé

2 cups cooked rice	2 eggs, separated
1½ cups milk	1 cup cold smoked fish flakes
2 tbsp. oil	Salt, pepper, paprika

Beat yolks and whites of eggs separately. Add fish flakes, milk, rice, butter, and seasonings. Blend thoroughly and fold into the beaten egg whites. Pour into greased baking dish and set in a pan of hot water. Bake 34 minutes at 350 degrees F. Serve with or without white sauce.

Smoked Fish and Scalloped Potatoes

2 cups flaked smoked fish	1 cup smoked fish stock
4 tbsp. cooking oil	2 cups cold potatoes
1 tsp. Tabasco	4 tbsp. flour
1 cup milk	1 tbsp. lemon juice
Pepper to taste	

Blend oil, fish stock, seasonings, and liquids into a smooth creamy sauce. In a greased casserole make alternate layers of fish and potatoes and cream sauce. Pour balance of sauce over top and bake until brown.

Smoke Fish Croquettes

2 cups flaked fish	2 eggs
1 cup mashed potatoes	1 clove garlic mashed and
1½ tsp. salt	rubbed inside bowl
⅛ tsp. pepper	Bread crumbs

Mix potatoes, salt, pepper, fish flakes, and 1 beaten egg. Form into croquettes and roll in fine bread crumbs. In the second well-beaten egg, add a little water, roll the croquettes again, adding more dry crumbs. Deep fry in oil or fat until browned. Serve hot.

Smoked Salmon Burgers

1 pound smoked flaked salmon	¼ cup chopped parsley
½ cup chopped onion	1 tsp. powdered mustard
¼ cup butter or oil	½ tsp. salt
⅓ cup dry bread crumbs	2 eggs beaten
6 round buttered buns	

Cook onion in butter until tender. Mix crumbs, egg, parsley, mustard, salt, and salmon. Shape into 6 cakes and roll in crumbs. Place cakes in a frying pan with a good layer of hot oil, not smoking. Fry until brown on one side, then turn and do the same on the other. Place cakes between buns, which have been warmed. Serve with lemon.

Smoked Florentine Salmon

1 lb. smoked salmon	3 tbsp. flour
1 cup cooked, drained spinach	¼ tsp. salt
4 tbsp. butter or margarine	1¼ cup milk
2 tbsp. sherry	¼ tsp. pepper
¼ cup grated Parmesan cheese	Dash nutmeg
2 tabsp. chopped onion	3 hard-cooked eggs, sliced
1 clove garlic, chopped fine	Watercress

Mash salmon and chop spinach. Mix spinach with 2 tbsp. butter, nutmeg, and pepper. Spread the mixture in a greased 8-inch round baking dish, 2 inches deep. Cook onion and garlic in 2 tbsp. butter. Blend in flour and salt. Mix with milk and cook until thick, stirring. Add sherry and salmon. Spread over spinach mixture in baking dish. Sprinkle with cheese. Bake at 350 degrees F. or moderate oven for 20 to 25 minutes. Garnish with egg slices and watercress. Serves 6.

Finnish Smoked Salmon Appetizers

Sliced smoked salmon	2 medium cucumbers
¼ cup salt	½ cup sour cream
3 tbsp. vinegar	1 tsp. salt
1½ tbsp. minced chives	Dash pepper
¾ tsp. dried dill seed	Dash hot pepper sauce
Buttered pumpernickel bread	

Peel and slice cucumbers thin. Sprinkle with salt. Let stand briefly, then rinse in cold water and drain. Mix sour cream with vinegar, chives, dill seed, salt, pepper, and pepper sauce. Combine with cucumber slices in a bowl. Chill for a couple of hours. Serve with thin slices of smoked salmon and triangles of buttered pumpernickel.

Smoked Columbia Sturgeon Bits

Put a pound of smoked sturgeon through food chopper. For every 2 cups of ground sturgeon use:

½ cup cracker crumbs	1 tsp. chopped onion
1 egg	Pinch of grated garlic
Salt and pepper	

Knead into small balls and roll in flour. Deep-fry until golden brown. Remove and simmer for 1 hour in 1 cup water. Serve hot or cold with toothpicks or spears.

Smoked Salmon Rollups

½ lb. smoked salmon	1 tbsp. salad dressing
1 tsp. hot horseradish	1 dash cayenne pepper
2 tbsp. lemon juice	1 package pastry paprika
1 tbsp. grated onion	2 tbsp. mayonnaise

Flake salmon; add horseradish, lemon juice, onion, salad dressing, mayonnaise, and pepper. Stir into a paste. Use paprika according to directions on package. Spread salmon mixture and roll into thin patties — or cut patties into small wedge-shaped pieces and roll from wide end to point. Bake on greased sheet in a hot oven at 425 degrees F. for 15 minutes or until light brown. Remove, sprinkle with paprika, and serve.

Smoked Salmon Dip

To 1 cup of thick sour cream add 1½ to 2 cups of flaked smoked or kippered salmon or steelhead. Add garlic salt to taste. Blend and let stand an hour or so in refrigerator before serving.

Smoked Louis

1 lb. smoked salmon	1 head lettuce
2 tomatoes, cut or sliced	2 hard-cooked egg yolks, sieved

Louis dressing

Flake salmon. Shred lettuce and place in a shallow salad bowl. Arrange salmon over the lettuce and place tomatoes around edges. Serve with Louis dressing.

To make *Louis Dressing:*

½ cup mayonnaise or salad oil	2 hard-cooked egg whites,
2 tbsp. whipping cream	chopped
2 tbsp. chili sauce	1 tbsp. chopped olives
2 tbsp. chopped green pepper	½ tsp. lemon juice
2 tbsp. chopped green onion	Dash salt

Dash pepper

Combine all ingredients and chill. Serves 6.

Smoked Salmon Hotcakes

1 cup pancake mix	1 egg
1 cup milk	1 tbsp. salad oil
½ lb. smoked salmon	White sauce

Flake salmon. Combine all ingredients except the salmon and white sauce. Stir the pancake batter until smooth, then add half the salmon. Prepare griddle and oil lightly. Fry each hotcake until golden brown. Add the rest of the salmon to the prepared white sauce and serve over the hotcakes. Instead of white sauce, any suitable sauce may be used — even some sour cream mixed with the remaining salmon and spread over the hotcakes. A novel variation is to top the hotcakes with a syrup of cooked cumquats.

Smoked Salmon Pie

2 eggs, slightly beaten	1 cup milk
1 lb. smoked salmon, flaked	½ cup soft bread crumbs
1 tsp. grated onion	¼ tsp. salt
½ tbsp. chopped parsley	1 tsp. lemon juice
½ tsp. garlic salt	

Mix all the ingredients in convenient order. Pour into greased 8-inch pie pan and bake in a moderate oven at 350 degrees F. for 45 minutes. Serves 6. For a deep-dish salmon pie, add potatoes, small onions, and green pea soup. Use to top hot biscuits.

Smoked Alaska Sandwiches

1 large can smoked salmon	½ cup chopped onion
½ cup chopped dill pickles	1 tbsp. chopped parsley
½ tsp. celery seed	Lettuce and mayonnaise

Flake salmon; add parsley, onion, celery seed, and chopped pickles. Mix with mayonnaise to suit and spread on toasted bread with lettuce if desired.

Alaska Louie

For a delicious salad meal, use the same ingredients as in the Smoked Alaska Sandwiches, with chunks of lettuce, slices of tomatoes, and gobs of cottage cheese.

Astoria Smoked Flakes

1½ cups smoked lingcod or sea bass (rockfish)	
2 cups whole milk	4 tbsp. cooking oil
4 tbsp. flour	½ tsp. Worcestershire
Pepper to taste	

Make a cream sauce of oil, flour, and milk; blend in seasonings. Mix with fish flakes. Put in individual ramekins and heat in oven. Garnish with pimento.

Hard Hat Pie

1 lb. smoked sausage	1 large can pork and beans
1 medium onion chopped	½ cup molasses

Stir into bean pot and cook in a moderate oven for about 30 minutes. Add sausage either whole or in bite-size chunks. Return to oven for another 30 minutes. Serves 6.

Hearty Chafing Dish

1 lb. smoked sausage	½ cup currant jelly
½ cup chili sauce	1½ tsp. prepared mustard
1½ tbsp. lemon juice	1 large can pineapple chunks

Slice sausage into bite-sized pieces. Drain pineapple chunks. Mix all ingredients in a saucepan and simmer for 15 minutes. Serve in a chafing dish with tidbit spears.

Sweet and Sour

1½ lbs. smoked sausage	1 cup pineapple juice
1 large can pineapple chunks	1 cup vinegar
½ cup soy sauce	1½ cups sugar
4 tbsp. cornstarch	1 cup water

Mix liquid and cornstarch in saucepan. Cook 10 minutes over low heat until thick. Add pineapple chunks and sausage which has been cut into bit-size chunks. Simmer 15 minutes. Serve hot.

Smoked Spanish Sausage

1½ lbs. smoked sausage	½ tsp. salt
1 No. 2 can tomato juice	Dash of pepper
½ cup chopped onion	1½ tsp. sugar
½ cup chopped green pepper	Dash of tabasco
½ cup chopped celery	Grated Parmesan cheese

Put sausage in skillet and add onion, tomato juice, celery, and seasonings. Simmer for an hour. Sprinkle with cheese and serve.

Smoked Sausage and Sauerkraut

1 lb. smoked sausage	½ pint water
1 can sauerkraut	1 potato, grated
1 tbsp. cooking oil	Salt and sugar to taste
2 onions, chopped	

Heat oil in skillet and fry chopped onions. Add sauerkraut and simmer a few minutes. Add the water and sausage and cook until done. Add the grated potato, salt, and sugar. Cook 45 minutes.

Scalloped Potatoes and Sausage

1 lb. smoked sausage	6 medium potatoes
1 medium onion	Salt and pepper
Flour	Milk
Butter or margarine	

Wash and peel potatoes and slice very thin. Place in baking dish. Fill dish two-thirds full with layers of potato slices and sliced onions. Sprinkle each layer with salt, pepper, flour, and dots of butter. Add milk until almost covered. Cover dish and place in 350 degree oven for 45 minutes. Remove, place sausages over the top, and return to oven for 15 or 20 minutes.

Grandma's Cocktail Dip

6 oz. cream cheese	1 clove garlic
2 cups flaked smoked fish	3 tbsp. minced onion
¼ tsp. salt	2 tbsp. Worcestershire
1 tbsp. lemon or lime juice	Pimento strips

Blend cheese and fish with the seasonings. Chill. Garnish with pimento when serving.

Smoked Shrimp Dish

1 pint smoked shrimp	1½ cups sharp cheddar, grated
2 cups sliced mushrooms	¾ cup chopped green onion
½ lb. cooked macaroni	1 pint sour cream
1 tbsp. onion powder	1 tbsp. curry powder
1 tbsp. lemon or lime juice	½ cube butter or margarine

Sauté mushrooms in butter; add curry powder and onion powder. Mix sour cream and lemon juice with a cup of grated cheese. Add shrimp and onions. Drain the macaroni and blend with mushrooms and sour cream in a casserole. Sprinkle with remaining cheese and bake at 375 degrees F. for 30 minutes.

Smoked Manhattan Chowder

1½ lbs. smoked fish	1 cup cooked tomatoes
1 medium chopped onion	2 cups water
3 cups milk	¼ cup flour
1 tsp. fish seasoning	Dash Tabasco

Simmer for 20 minutes the combined smoked fish, onion, tomatoes, and water. In a separate container blend flour, milk, and seasonings. Cook until thickened. Blend the two mixtures and serve hot.

This recipe can also be used New England style without the tomatoes. Add more milk.

Norwegian Fishburgers

1 lb. smoked salmon or cod	1 cup chopped onion
2 tbsp. cooking oil	2 cups mashed potatoes
¼ cup parsley, chopped	1 egg, well beaten
½ cup bread crumbs	Dash pepper

In a hot skillet cook onion in oil. Mix all ingredients except bread crumbs and make into cakes. Roll cakes in the crumbs and fry in hot oil until one side is brown. Turn and brown the other side. Drain and make burgers with hot buttered buns or sourdough bread.

To make real Old Country fishburgers, use an oil garlic sauce spread on the bread.

To make *oil garlic sauce*: (Can be used with many other dishes.)

To 1 pint of cooking oil add 1 tablespoon salt, 1 teaspoon black pepper, 1 tablespoon Worcestershire sauce or beef extract, and 3 cloves of garlic, minced. Place in a mason jar with lid and shake well, or mix in blender.

Creole Smoked Tongue

Slice smoked tongue into half-inch cuts and mix with a No. 2 can of tomatoes, 2 large onions minced or chopped, 3 stalks of celery, and a cup of warm water. Simmer and season to taste when the vegetables are tender.

Smoked Camp Cutlets

The tenderloin cuts of deer, elk, and antelope or of domestic beef, pork, and lamb work best. After smoking, rub pieces with onion and garlic and slice into cutlets, very thin. Rub with bacon drippings, butter, or cooking oil, and skewer over patio broiler. Season with salt and pepper. When done, make a sandwich of hot buttered French bread. As indicated, this dish can be adapted to home or camp use. In camp a green stick can be used for a skewer and a bed of campfire coals for cooking.

Smoked and Breaded Brains

Dip smoked brains in beaten egg, roll in cracker crumbs, and fry in bacon drippings. Season with salt and pepper to taste. The smoked brains can also be minced and mixed with chopped onions or chives; add to beaten eggs and scramble.

Scalloped Fish Rice

2 cups smoked flaked fish	3 eggs well beaten
2 cups cooked rice	Paprika, pepper, and pimento
1 cup milk	strips
3 tbsp. butter or margarine	

Mix fish flakes and rice and place in greased baking dish. Combine the seasonings, milk, and eggs and pour over mixture. Lay strips of pimento on top and serve with relish or pickles.

Don's Special Hot Seafood Dip

This seems like a good place to reveal my own special sauce. It can be used on any seafood plate.

½ cup catsup	1 tsp. Worcestershire
½ cup chili sauce	3 tbsp. lemon juice
1 tsp. grated onion	¼ tsp. salt
1 tbsp. horseradish	3 drops liquid hot pepper sauce
1 tbsp. mayonnaise	Dash pepper

Mix all ingredients and place in a handy location.

How To Light An Outdoor Grill

Line the bottom of the outdoor barbecue grill with heavy aluminum foil. Place a layer of pebbles or vermiculite on this, so the fire can breath. Place a layer of charcoal briquets on top of this. Then make a small stack of briquets in the middle. Soak charcoal with a recommended liquid lighting fluid, or place solid fuel starter at strategic places in the briquets. Light and let burn until coals glow, then spread coals out evenly. When the surface of the coals is covered with a gray ash, the fire is ready for use.

Smoky Flavor Cooking

A tangy smoke flavor can be imparted to any outdoor cooking. Use wood chips of apple, oak, maple, hickory, or cherry, or even corncobs. Soak chips in water about an hour before using. When cooking, add a few chips at a time to the charcoal coals. If the chips flare up into flames, use more water to dampen. On a gas grill, scatter wet chips on the ceramic briquets for a strong smoke flavor. For a more subtle flavor, wrap the chips in perforated foil first.

IV

HOW TO MAKE JERKY AND PEMMICAN

Jerking Means Drying

In the old days before refrigeration, jerking was the standard frontier method of curing or processing fresh meat. A mountain man could kill a deer or elk, butcher it, and have the meat jerked almost faster than you could set the table.

Nowadays it is even easier than in Kit Carson's day, and infinitely better. For one thing you don't even have to kill your own meat. You can do your hunting in the neighborhood butcher shop or supermarket.

But first, just so you'll know what you're talking about, let's start with a historical definition. Jerky is merely an Anglocized version of the old Spanish word *charqui*, which simply means dried meat or dried beef. In other words, it's just a method of drying red meat.

Note carefully that I said *dried* and not *cooked* meat. Cooked meat will spoil rapidly without refrigeration or salting. Dried without cooking — in other words, dehydrated — it will keep indefinitely with or without refrigeration. (But not around our house where we eat it up as fast as we make it!)

Well, that's enough palaver. Let's get started.

First you need the meat. It takes about 5 pounds of fresh meat to make 1 pound of jerky. The meat can be beef, buffalo (yes, you can buy buffalo now, raised on western ranches and federal wildlife refuges), elk, deer, bear, caribou, reindeer (you can also buy this), or musk oxen. The acquisition of suitable meat is between you and your resources. Any red, lean meat will do. All fat and membrane *must be removed* from any meat, along with

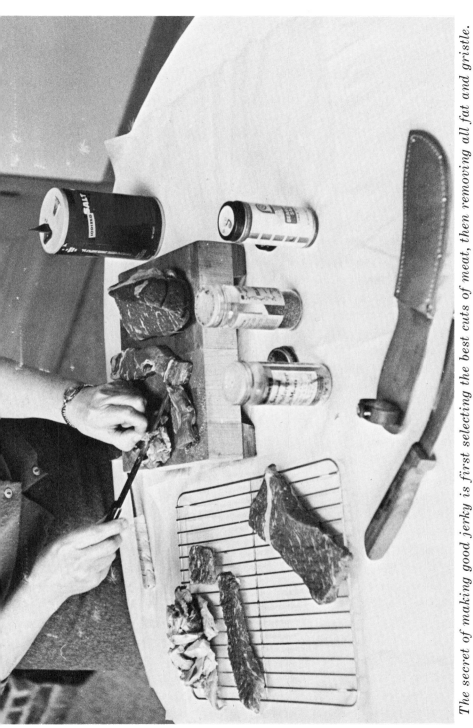

The secret of making good jerky is first selecting the best cuts of meat, then removing all fat and gristle.

the bones. The rule is: The better the meat, the better the jerky.

During the Lewis and Clark Expedition of 1803-1806, literally tons of wild game were consumed by the corps; all that could not be consumed on the spot was dried or jerked for later use. This was done by slicing the meat into thin strips and hanging it in the sun or in the smoke of the campfire for several days. If the jerky was not ready by the time they broke camp, they simply packed it up and hung it again at the next campsite.

If you want to do it this way, have plenty of salt and pepper handy. Cut the meat into ¼-inch strips and hang it in the sun or any dry place where the water content can be evaporated. First soak the strips in salt water for an hour or so. On the seacoast, sea water can be used for this. Rinse with fresh water before hanging, pat dry, and sprinkle generously with pepper. The pepper not only gives it flavor but helps keep the flies off, too.

Build a smoky fire under the hanging meat and let the smoke and wind do the work. If it looks like rain, take the meat down to protect it, and hang it up again when the coast is clear.

At home, one method is to prepare a seasoning mix of salt, pepper, oregano, marjoram, basil, garlic powder, seasoning smoke, or what-have-you. Pound this into the strips and place the strips on a tray or rack in the oven. Set the heat on "warm." Leave the oven door ajar so the moisture-laden air can escape. Be careful not to cook the meat as it is drying. The process takes several hours. When ready, the meat strips will have shriveled up and often turned black, or at least mahogany brown. Remove and let the trays stand where the meat will cool. If properly dried, the strips will be flexible enough to bend without snapping. Venison turns blacker than domestic beef, but when completely dry the meat is ready to eat no matter what the color is.

Smoked jerky can be made by placing the strips in the smoke or smokehouse over alder, fruitwood, or hickory

Work salt and seasoning into the strips of meat as they are sliced, pound thoroughly.

chips for a couple of hours, finishing the meat off in the oven. The entire jerking process can be done in the smoker, of course, but the oven method is much easier and cheaper.

Another version of smoked jerky is made by first brining the strips in a solution of ½ pound of salt to 1 gallon of water in a crock, plastic bowl, granite pail, or wooden barrel. *Do not use a metallic container for brine solutions.*

Weight the meat down so the liquid covers the surface and let it stand for 12 hours. Or you can make the solution of half salt and half brown sugar, spiced with condiments to taste.

Here's a good standard jerky brine:

1 cup curing salt	1 tsp. liquid garlic
½ cup brown sugar or molasses	2 quarts of water
4 tbsp. black pepper	

Use the above proportions to make enough brine to cover the meat or fowl.

After brining anywhere from 8 to 10 hours, remove meat and rinse each piece in clean, fresh water, such as under the cold water tap. Pat dry with paper towels to remove excess moisture. Let stand to air-dry for an hour or so. Then rub in the seasonings of your choice, such as onion salt, garlic salt, pepper, or a prepared seasoning mix that can be obtained from the spice department at the market.

Next, smoke the meat for 8 to 12 hours or until ready. Test by twisting a strip of meat. It should be flexible but stiff like a piece of rope. Remove and let stand until cool.

Jerky can be made from lamb brisket and turkey in the same way. To make the turkey jerky, slice the bird and follow the above directions.

Smokehouse Jerky

After brining according to preference, drain well and place trays of meat strips in smokehouse. Let the smoke

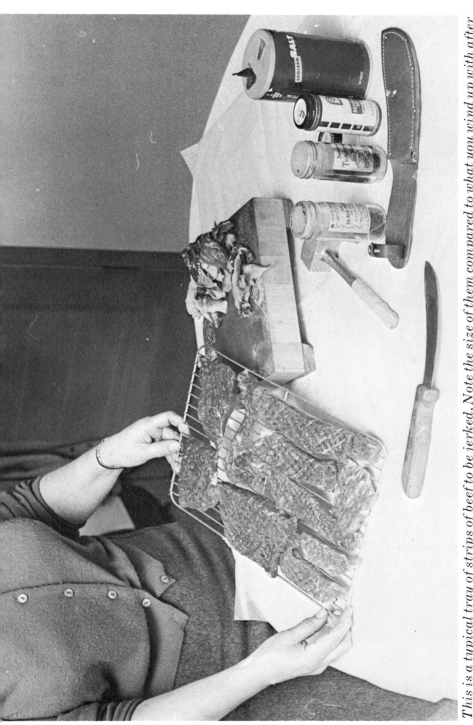

This is a typical tray of strips of beef to be jerked. Note the size of them compared to what you wind up with after jerking.

dry and flavor the strips for 5 to 15 days, depending on the meat and weather conditions. Alder is my favorite wood, but maple, ash, apple or cherry wood, hickory, or even corncobs are excellent. When finished, store in airtight containers or in the refrigerator. If all the fat has been removed, the jerky will keep indefinitely even without refrigeration. This method is especially good for big game.

Dry Brining

With this method, make a mixture of half salt and half brown sugar (some stores handle a commercially prepared sugar-cure mixture and brining salt), plus herbs and condiments to suit. Rub this mixture thoroughly into the meat. Place in crock (without water) and weight down. The moisture will gradually seep out to the bottom of the crock. This is called "horsing." Allow to stand overnight or longer, until most of the moisture is drained out. Rinse in cold, fresh water and place in smokehouse for 12 hours or more.

Domestic Meats

Here's a tried and proven brine for all domestic meats: Mix 2 cups salt, 1 cup brown sugar, 1 cup cider, 1 teaspoon cloves, 1 teaspoon black pepper, ½ teaspoon garlic, and ½ gallon of water. Bring to boil, dunk the meat in the brine for a period equal to 5 minutes per pound. Remove and rinse in fresh, cold water. Let stand until dry. Place in smoker and cure for 6 to 12 hours. Finish off in a warm oven with door open if quicker results are desired.

Jerky Venison

Venison means not only deer meat but any kind of red-meated game. To make jerky venison in the oven, remove all the fat from about 3 pounds of meat (deer, elk, or just plain beef) and slice very thin. Add some liquid smoke to one side, then salt both sides generously. Place the strips in layers in a large crock or bowl and lightly pepper each layer as stacked. Let stand for about 6 hours or even overnight. Remove, place strips in oven on racks with plenty of space around each piece of meat. Set the oven on warm or about 150 degrees F. with the door open. Let dry for about 10 to 12 hours. Store in a dry, airtight container. If a moist type of jerky is desired, store in refrigerator.

Kippered Jerky

Smoked or kippered jerky may be prepared with most game and domestic meats. First remove all fat and gristle. Cut into strips not over ½ inch thick. Place meat in layers in nonmetallic containers, liberally salting down each layer. If tough cuts of meat are used, sprinkle powdered meat tenderizer on each layer. At this time, add pepper, garlic powder, Tabasco, brown sugar, or any other flavoring or spices desired. Set container in a cool place for at least 18 hours. Remove meat and drain thoroughly. Place strips in smoker for the length of time needed to produce the degree of jerky wanted — moist or completely dry.

Blanched Jerky

Here's a quick and easy way to make jerky from big game. Blanch or parboil the strips of lean meat, cut about ¾ inch thick and 6 inches long. Cut the strips lengthwise with the muscle, not across the grain.

Blanch in a solution of 2 cups of salt per gallon of boiling water with pepper to suit. Drop the strips into this boiling mixture for only a minute or less. Remove and drain, then place the strips in the smokehouse or oven (the latter only if you don't want the strips smoked).

Smoke for 3 to 5 hours. If you like a spicy jerky, pepper or season to taste before smoking.

With this method you can also combine the smokehouse and oven process. Smoke the meat for a while, then place in the oven to finish off.

Jerked goat

Many small-boat voyagers, who have had to live off the land in remote parts of the world, have discovered a way to preserve goat meat, even in the tropics. Many of the lonely islands are overrun with wild — or more correctly, feral — goats, left there in the old sailing-ship days for the benefit of castaways. They are easy to hunt and when properly butchered furnish excellent fresh meat. To make goat jerky, cut the lean portions into strips about ¼ inch thick, 2 inches wide, and about a foot long. Rub lemon on the meat or use reconstituted lemon or lime juice. Rub salt on meat thoroughly and then hang up to dry in the sun until ready, protecting from flies or insects.

The meat can be eaten raw or cooked (after first beating the strips until they shred). Put meat in a frying pan with cooking oil or lard and pieces of onion and garlic. Slowly add tomato sauce or puree and a little water. Let simmer for a half hour or so.

They call this *machaca* along the coast of Central America, where I first saw it made.

The dried strip jerky will keep for weeks without cooking.

Cascades Jerky

This method was used by an old prospector I once knew in the region that is now the North Cascades National Park in Washington state. Cut strips of deer meat about an inch thick, a foot long, and 2 inches wide. Remove all fat and membrane. Do not use any water. Mix 2

Some like to blanch the strips of meat before jerking, by dunking briefly in boiling water. They may have to be re-seasoned afterwards.

tablespoons of black pepper with a pound of salt. If desired, add allspice or cinnamon to the mixture. Rub this curing mixture into the meat and dust on more of same.

Hang the pieces of meat in the open air where the breeze can touch them with the gentle kiss of the high mountains. Do not hang in the direct rays of the sun. This is the real slow method, and it takes about a month to complete the curing. Take the meat down every night to protect it from ravaging animals, and hang it up each morning. Protect from insects with cheesecloth if necessary.

When it is ready to eat, you will taste the ultimate in all forms of jerky.

More Jerky

As you may have guessed from reading all this, jerking, like smoking, is an art with as many different methods as there are practitioners. Basically, one should strive for either a moist or a dry product, depending upon taste and upon how long one wants the jerky to keep without refrigeration. In the matter of taste, there is also room for much experimentation. In addition to the spices listed here, one can also use Worcestershire or Tabasco sauce, or even A-1 Sauce.

One can also obtain seasonings already conveniently mixed at any well-stocked store. Preparations such as Morton's Sugar Cure and Morton's Tender-Quick also help make things easier for the beginner.

Another important point to remember is that the amount of salt used should vary with the thickness of the strips. On large pieces or chunks use a lot of salt; on small, thin strips, use salt more sparingly. If too much salt is used on the latter, they tend to dry out too quickly and are too salty to the taste.

The strips can also be seasoned after drying — especially if they don't taste just right. Lay them out and paint them with a mixture of catsup and vinegar, to which you can add Tabasco or Worcestershire. I like light-smoked jerky painted with A-1 Sauce, but that's just my personal preference. Experiment by seasoning pieces of the same batch with different flavors.

The finished jerky can be stored in plastic bags or glass mason jars. Properly stored, the strips will keep for months and even years.

Pemmican

The French-Canadian *voyageurs*, who paddled their canoes regularly across the continent carrying freight and furs, practically lived on pemmican. Packed in 50-pound skins, pemmican was even a medium of exchange in many areas.

Pemmican is jerky that has been pounded into a coarse meal and mixed with tallow, bear grease, suet, and dried berries. It is a near-perfect trail food or survival ration, with practically all the nutrients needed for hard physical life in the outdoors — except vitamin C, which can be added by grinding some wild rose hips into the mixture.

The federal government spent hundreds of thousands of dollars researching pemmican for use by the armed forces as a survival food during and between recent wars — and the results are filed away somewhere in the Pentagon archives. Some mail-order houses catering to mountaineers offer pemmican at prices approaching that of platinum, and the product in many cases is a pitiful substitute for the real thing.

To make pemmican, chop up some strips of jerky, mix with dried berries or raisins, and grind the whole mess in the kitchen grinder. Mix with melted beef suet and stuff in sausage skins or some handy container. I almost said plastic bags, but I would be careful using these. The original pemmican was stuffed into bags made of deerskin and sometimes of the intestinal tubes of buffalo. For flavor you can use raisins, currents, cranberries, serviceberries, or elderberries.

Pemmican, like jerky, will keep indefinitely without refrigeration.

Eatin' Jerky

It shouldn't really need any explanation, but many readers have asked me how you eat jerky, once made. The answer is simple: Bite off a chunk and start chewing. Let the chunk work around in your mouth so your juices start working and you begin to savor the delicate tang. Only then will you believe that meat does not have to be cooked to be delicious and nutritious.

Not only is it nutritious, but with a pocketful of jerky and some water you can travel for several days on foot in an emergency. It is also a good snack food for taking into the office. After all, survival is also a major consideration in many modern offices, isn't it?

Old Codger Jerky

An old mountain man I know, who is a mite too lazy to bother with a regular smokehouse, has a specific method for making his jerky:

Cut meat into 1-inch-thick strips. Make a mix of half salt and half brown sugar, with black pepper to suit. Place in a cake pan. Dredge each piece of meat in the dry mix and pack into a crock or glass jar. Weight down and let stand for 3 days. Remove meat from crock and rinse in cold water. Dry thoroughly. Mix liquid smoke and more pepper in a large bowl and paint the pieces of meat with a pastry brush. Hang up to dry for about a week. Then place in plastic bags and store in freezer. (My friend has no freezer, so he eats his jerky right away.)

Smoking the strips in the smoker after seasoning greatly adds to the taste and quality of jerky. For final curing, they can be placed in a warm oven with the door ajar, to complete the dehydration process.

Basic Jerky

Still another way to make jerky is used by another backwoods acquaintance. Make a mixture of ½ cup salt, ½ tablespoon garlic salt, and ½ tablespoon pepper. Cut meat into 2-inch-wide strips, 1 inch thick. Roll strips in seasoning, or "dredge" as the television cooks say. Place meat in a crock and weight down with a plate. Brine this way for 5 days, then remove and rinse. Dry and place in smoker. Smoke about 18 hours or until the meat is a purple color when you cut into it. At this point you can rub garlic powder into it, if you like.

A variation of this is to mix the brine ingredients with 1 quart of water, bring to a boil, and place the meat in the boiling mixture for 10 minutes. Remove and place immediately in the smoker.

Fish Pemmican

I don't recommend this, for the simple reason that the process is not necessary these days — as it was during the frontier days and before. For centuries the Indians on the middle Columbia River at Celilo Falls processed salmon this way. The squaws first dried the split carcasses in the sun, then pounded the flesh into granulated form, mixed it with an oil obtained from the head of the steelhead, and packed this fish pemmican into baskets made of beargrass and lined with fish skins.

These baskets held about 90 to 100 pounds of pemmican, which took from 500 to 600 pounds of fresh fish to make. The baskets were used in the thriving commerce between the river tribes and the inland mountain tribes. Also, for tribal use, the baskets could be buried and the fish would remain edible for several years.

Capt. William Clark wrote in his journal, during the party's stay at Celilo Falls, that one pile of these baskets full of fish pemmican amounted to about 100,000 pounds. An estimated 18 million pounds of pemmican was put up annually at Celilo, or more than a million fresh-caught salmon a year.

Survival Pemmican

The *voyageurs* of the old Canadian West, who paddled canoes from Montreal to the Columbia supplying the posts and returning with furs, practically lived on pemmican. This pemmican was a high-calorie ration; a typical daily allowance came close to 6,000 calories. This is far more than the average person today needs to maintain weight and a balanced metabolism. Those who spend much time outdoors in northern climates skiing, hunting, and engaging in other physical pursuits, may need as much as 5,000 calories a day. A typical pemmican, such as used by the military for survival packs, would be made up as follows:

33 percent beef suet	5 percent soybean grits
20 percent whole milk powder	2 percent oatmeal
18 percent dry bacon bits	2 percent dehydrated pea soup
5 percent dehydrated beef liver	2 percent dehydrated potatoes
5 percent dried beef	1 percent bouillon powder
5 percent dehydrated tomato concentrate	1 percent brewer's yeast

Small amounts of onion salt, paprika, lemon powder, caraway seed, cayenne pepper, black pepper

In normal use the above pemmican formula would be part of a trail ration which would include milk chocolate, powdered cocoa, lump sugar, quick-cooking oatmeal, nuts, dried fruit, whole milk powder, bacon, biscuits, butter, and salt and pepper.

With this daily ration of about 2 pounds per person per day, one could maintain body weight even under Arctic conditions and physical labor.

APPENDIX

REFERENCES

For Drying

The astonishing boom in home-drying which began in the early 1970s resulted in a proliferation of small manufacturing firms specializing in equipment all over the country. Many of these are backyard operations or part-time enterprises which may disappear as quickly as they sprouted like mushrooms in a wet pasture. Most state agricultural college extension services will have plans or leaflets on home-drying or curing. The homemaker section of Sunday newspapers, and home-and-family type magazines often carry articles on the subject. The Yellow Pages of the telephone book are another source of information. The following sources are offered as suggestions, without any specific endorsement given or implied:

Agriculture Handbook No. 8, *Composition of Foods*, U.S. Department of Agriculture. This book is an invaluable source and should be first on any list.

Home Drying of Fruits and Vegetables, Extension Service, Utah State University, Logan, UT 84322.

How to Build a Portable Electric Food Dehydrator, Extension Circular 855, Extension Service, Oregon State University, Corvallis, OR 97331.

For Smoking and Jerking

A Cardboard Smokehouse, Rust, Walter A., U.S. Department of Interior, Fish and Wildlife Service, Fishery Leaflet 204, 1946.

Game Foods, Cooperative Extension Service, Oregon State University, Extension bulletin 790, Corvallis, OR, 1967.

Home Preservation of Fishery Products, Jarvis, N. D., U.S. Department of Interior, U.S. Fish and Wildlife Services, Fishery Leaflet 18, April, 1945.

The Nitty-Gritty of Smoke-Cooking, Stair, Dan, Luhr Jensen and Sons, Inc., Hood River, OR Leaflet.

The Old-Fashioned Dutch Oven Cookbook, Holm, Don, Caxton Printers, Ltd., Caldwell, Idaho, 1969.

Portable Barbecue Box and Fish Cooker, Washington State Department of Fisheries, Olympia, WA, 1957.

A Practical Small Smokehouse for Fish, U.S. Department of Commerce, Bureau of Commercial Fisheries, Oct. 1917.

The Smoke-Curing of Fish and the Application of a Controlled Method to the Process, Anderson, Clarence L., and Robert K. Pederson, Tech. Report No. 1, Washington State Department of Fisheries, 1947.

A Smokehouse for the Sportsman and Hobbyist, Cooperative Extension Service, Oregon State University, Bulletin 788, Corvallis OR, 1966.

SOURCES OF SUPPLY

Dryers

Harvest Mills, 28230 S. Oglesby Rd., Canby, OR 97013.

Sunshine Foods, Box 248, Edmonds, WA 98020. A source of drying and related equipment, as well as bulk dried foods.

United Vito-Way, P.O. Box 2216, Everett, WA 98203. This is a good source for food dryers, juicers, water distillers, and related items.

Smokers

Small, portable electric smokers can now be purchased in various models and sizes from most well-stocked sporting goods stores, hardware stores, and mail-order houses.

One of the best of the small home-smokers is the Little Chief, manufactured by Luhr Jensen and Sons, Hood River, Oregon. This firm can also supply wood chips and other accessories.

Coloring

Commercial smoked-fish processors usually use a dye to impart that rich salmon color to kippered fish. It gives the finished product a more desirable appearance but has no effect whatever on the taste or keeping qualities. The dye is usually 150 Orange I, an aniline dye approved by the Federal Food and Drug Administration. It can be obtained from meat and butcher supply houses.

The proportion most commonly used is 3 to 4 ounces of dye to 20 gallons of water. The dye should first be dissolved in a small amount of water, then mixed with the remainder. Fish chunks are dipped in the dye solution for 15 to 30 seconds.

Miscellaneous supplies

Pickling mixtures, such as the kind pumped into hams and shoulders with a long hypodermic needle in commercial houses, can be obtained from butcher supply companies listed in the Yellow Pages. These firms can also supply crocks and hypodermics.

MEAT PROCESSING

Aging

Never age pork. Freeze it as soon as possible after chilling. Only good beef and lamb should be aged before cutting up for storage. Low grade, lean meat will shrink excessively if aged. This may, however, be desirable in the case of making jerky. In any case, aging is merely holding or storing the carcass at 34 to 38 degrees for 7 to 10 days before cutting it up.

Freezing

Quick-freezing is desirable for fish and meat of all kinds. Slow freezing breaks down the muscle cells and permits loss of natural body juices when thawed. Freeze at temperatures as low as possible. store meat at zero or lower to prevent development of rancidity. The storage temperature should not vary. Fluctuations in temperature cause dehydration.

Meat yield from carcasses

Many people who do a lot of home smoking and curing economize by buying their meat and fish in wholesale quantities or at locker meat discounts. If convenient to rural areas, whole or half carcasses can be purchased at real savings (check with local regulations first). Even if buying locker beef already cut, it is educational to know just what you are paying for. For instance, a 1,000-pound steer on the hoof yields only 590 pounds of good-to-choice beef when butchered. This is further reduced to about 465 pounds of retail cuts that are eatable.

A 145-pound pork carcass yields only about 109 pounds of eating meat. The retail packaged weight of a 200-pound veal is only 107 pounds; of a 90-pound lamb, only 33 pounds.

It takes 90 pounds of salmon "in the round," to yield 48 one-pound cans such as you buy off the shelf at the grocery store.

Smoking and drying fish and meat further reduces the eating weight, although in the case of jerky the meat is reconstituted to a degree by moisture when eaten or used in a recipe.

SALT TABLE

Salinometer Degrees	*Ounces Salt Per Gallon Water*
3.8	1.3
7.6	2.6
11.3	4.0
15.1	5.3
18.9	6.7
22.6	8.1
26.4	9.6
30.2	11.1
34.0	12.7
37.7	14.2
40.5	15.8
45.3	17.5
49.1	19.1
52.8	20.8
56.6	22.6
60.4	24.4
64.2	26.2
68.0	28.1
71.7	30.0
75.5	32.0
79.2	34.0
83.0	36.1
86.8	38.2
90.6	40.4
94.3	42.7
100.0	46.1

WATER CONTENT

The degree of water content is a critical factor in both smoking and jerking because it determines how much salt is necessary for curing and dehydrating. All fresh meat and fish contain large quantities of water. The following is typical:

Beef	60 percent
Veal	65 percent
Cheese	40 percent
Chicken	66 percent
Turkey	66 percent
Oily fish	70 percent
Whitefish	80 percent

MISCELLANEOUS TABLES

In an old trunk left by my mother when she died, I found bundles of recipes and related information. Among these were some tables of interest to the dedicated country-style homemaker.

Table of Proportions

4 even teaspoons of baking powder to 1 quart of flour
1 teaspoon of flavoring to 1 quart of custard
1 teaspoon of soda to 1 pint of sour milk
1 teaspoon extract of beef to 1 quart of water
1 teaspoon of mixed herbs to 1 quart of soup stock
1 teaspoon of salt to 2 quarts of flour
1 teaspoon of soda to 1 cup of molasses
1 tablespoon (each) of chopped vegetables to 1 quart of soup stock

Abbreviations

t = teaspoon	hr = hour
T = tablespoon	sm = small
c = cup	med = medium
pt = pint	lg = large
qt = quart	in = inch
gal = gallon	sq = square
oz = ounce	dz = dozen
lb = pound	pkg = package
min = minute	db = double

Weights and Measures

3 teaspoons = 1 tablespoon
2 tablespoons = 1 ounce
16 tablespoons of liquid = 1 cup
12 tablespoons dry = 1 cup
1 heaping quart of flour = 1 pound
1 pint granulated sugar = 1 pound
2 cups butter = 1 pound
1 pint brown sugar = 12 ounces
12 medium eggs = 1 pound
4 cups flour = 1 pound
2 teacups flour = 1 pint
4 tablespoons liquid = 1 wineglass
1 cup flour = 4 ounces
Butter, size of egg = 2 ounces
Butter, size of walnut = 1 ounce

Diabetic Note

Many of the recipes in this book which call for sugar, especially those in smoke curing, can successfully use Sugar Twin or a similar substitute, provided they have not been banned by the Food and Drug Administration.